Why Marx Was Right

Terry Eagleton is Bailrigg Distinguished Professor of English Literature, University of Lancaster. He is the author of more than forty books spanning the fields of literary theory, postmodernism, politics, ideology and religion. His most recent titles, *On Evil* and *Reason, Faith, and Revolution*, are published by Yale.

Why Marx Was Right

TERRY EAGLETON

Yale

UNIVERSITY PRESS

New Haven & London

Yale University Press books may be purchased in quantity for educational, business, or promotional use. For information, please e-mail sales.press@ yale.edu (U.S. office) or sales@yaleup.co.uk (U.K. office).

Designed by James J. Johnson and set in Granjon Roman type by Keystone Typesetting, Inc.

Printed in Great Britain by TJ International Ltd, Padstow, Cornwall

Library of Congress Cataloging-in-Publication Data

Eagleton, Terry, 1943–

Why Marx was right / Terry Eagleton.

p.   cm.

Includes bibliographical references and index.

ISBN 978-0-300-16943-0 (hardcover : alk. paper)

ISBN 978-0-300-18153-1 (cl: alk. paper)

1. Marx, Karl, 1818–1883. 2. Communism. 3. Capitalism. I. Title.

HX39.5E234   2011

335.4—dc22

2010041471

A catalogue record for this book is available from the British Library.

This paper meets the requirements of ANSI/NISO Z39.48–1992 (Permanence of Paper).

10   9   8   7   6   5   4   3

For Dom and Hadi

Contents

Preface

This book had its origin in a single, striking thought: What if all the most familiar objections to Marx's work are mistaken? Or at least, if not totally wrongheaded, mostly so?

This is not to suggest that Marx never put a foot wrong. I am not of that leftist breed that piously proclaims that everything is open to criticism, and then, when asked to produce three major criticisms of Marx, lapses into truculent silence. That I have my own doubts about some of his ideas should be clear enough from this book. But he was right enough of the time about enough important issues to make calling oneself a Marxist a reasonable self-description. No Freudian imagines that Freud never blundered, just as no fan of Alfred Hitchcock defends the master's every shot and line of screenplay. I am out to present Marx's ideas not as perfect but as plausible. To demonstrate this, I take in this book ten of the most standard criticisms of Marx, in no particular order of importance, and try to refute them one by one. In the process, I also aim to provide a clear, accessible introduction to his thought for those unfamiliar with his work.

The *Communist Manifesto* has been described as "without doubt the single most influential text written in the nineteenth century."[1] Very few thinkers, as opposed to statesmen, scientists, soldiers, religious figures and the like, have changed the course of actual history as decisively as its author. There are no Cartesian governments, Platonist guerilla fighters or Hegelian trade unions. Not even Marx's most implacable critics would deny that he transformed our understanding of human history. The antisocialist thinker Ludwig von Mises described socialism as "the most powerful reform movement that history has ever known, the first ideological trend not limited to a section of mankind but supported by people of all races, nations, religions and civilisations."[2] Yet there is a curious notion abroad that Marx and his theories can now be safely buried—and this in the wake of one of the most devastating crises of capitalism on historical record. Marxism, for long the most theoretically rich, politically uncompromising critique of that system, is now complacently consigned to the primeval past.

TERRY EAGLETON

That crisis has at least meant that the word "capitalism," usually disguised under some such coy pseudonym as "the modern age," "industrialism" or "the West," has become current once more. You can tell that the capitalist system is in trouble when people start talking about capitalism. It indicates that the system has ceased to be as natural as the air we breathe, and can be seen instead as the historically rather recent phenomenon that it is. Moreover, whatever was born can always die, which is why social systems like to present themselves as immortal. Rather as a bout of dengue fever makes you newly aware of your body, so a form of social life can be perceived for what it is when it begins to break down. Marx was the first to identify the historical object known as capitalism—to show how it arose, by what laws it worked, and how it might be brought to an end. Rather as Newton discovered the invisible forces known as the laws of gravity, and Freud laid bare the workings of an invisible phenomenon known as the unconscious, so Marx unmasked our everyday life to reveal an imperceptible entity known as the capitalist mode of production.

I say very little in this book about Marxism as a moral and cultural critique. This is because it is not generally raised as an objection to Marxism, and so does not fit my format. In my view, however, the extraordinarily rich, fertile body of Marxist writing in this vein is reason in itself to align oneself with the Marxist legacy. Alienation, the "commodification" of social life, a culture of greed, aggression, mindless hedonism and growing nihilism, the steady hemorrhage of meaning and value from human existence: it is hard to find an intelligent discussion of these questions that is not seriously indebted to the Marxist tradition.

In the early days of feminism, some maladroit if well-meaning male authors used to write "When I say 'men,' I mean of course 'men and women.'" I should point out in similar vein that when I say Marx, I quite often mean Marx and Engels. But the relationship between the two is another story.

I am grateful to Alex Callinicos, Philip Carpenter and Ellen Meiksins Wood, who read a draft of this book and made some invaluable criticisms and suggestions.

TERRY EAGLETON

Why Marx Was Right

ONE

Marxism is finished. It might conceivably have had some relevance to a world of factories and food riots, coal miners and chimney sweeps, widespread misery and massed working classes. But it certainly has no bearing on the increasingly classless, socially mobile, postindustrial Western societies of the present. It is the creed of those who are too stubborn, fearful or deluded to accept that the world has changed for good, in both senses of the term.

That Marxism is finished would be music to the ears of Marxists everywhere. They could pack in their marching and picketing, return to the bosom of their grieving families and enjoy an evening at home instead of yet another tedious committee meeting. Marxists want nothing more than to stop being Marxists. In this respect, being a Marxist is nothing like being a Buddhist or a billionaire. It is more like being a medic. Medics are perverse, self-thwarting creatures who do themselves out of a job by curing patients who then no longer need them. The task of political radicals, similarly, is to get to the point where they would no longer be necessary because their goals would have been accomplished. They would then be free to bow out, burn their Guevara posters, take up that long-neglected cello again and talk about something more intriguing than the Asiatic mode of production. If there are still Marxists or feminists around in twenty years' time, it will be a sorry prospect. Marxism is meant to be a strictly provisional affair, which is why anyone who invests the whole of their identity in it has missed the point. That there is a life after Marxism is the whole point of Marxism.

There is only one problem with this otherwise alluring vision. Marxism is a critique of capitalism—the most searching, rigorous, comprehensive critique of its kind ever to be launched. It is also the only such critique that has transformed large sectors of the globe. It follows, then, that as long as capitalism is still in business, Marxism must be as well. Only by superannuating its opponent can it superannuate itself. And on the last sighting, capitalism appeared as feisty as ever.

Most critics of Marxism today do not dispute the point. Their claim, rather, is that the system has altered almost unrecognizably since the days of Marx, and that this is why his ideas are no longer relevant. Before we examine this claim in more detail, it is worth noting that Marx himself was perfectly aware of the ever-changing nature of the system he challenged. It is to Marxism itself that we owe the concept of different historical forms of capital: mercantile, agrarian, industrial, monopoly, financial, imperial and so on. So why should the fact that capitalism has changed its shape in recent decades discredit a theory that sees change as being of its very essence? Besides, Marx himself predicted a decline of the working class and a steep increase in white-collar work. We shall be looking at this a little later. He also foresaw so-called globalisation—odd for a man whose thought is supposed to be archaic. Though perhaps Marx's "archaic" quality is what makes him still relevant today. He is accused of being outdated by the champions of a capitalism rapidly reverting to Victorian levels of inequality.

In 1976, a good many people in the West thought that Marxism had a reasonable case to argue. By 1986, many of them no longer considered that it had. What exactly had happened in the meanwhile? Was it simply that these people were now buried under a pile of toddlers? Had Marxist theory been unmasked as bogus by some world-shaking new research? Did we stumble upon a long-lost manuscript by Marx confessing that it was all a joke? It was not that we discovered to our dismay that Marx was in the pay of capitalism. This is because we knew it all along. Without the Ermen & Engels mill in Salford, owned by Friedrich Engels's textile-manufacturing father, the chronically impoverished Marx might well have not survived to pen polemics against textile manufacturers.

Something had indeed happened in the period in question. From the mid-1970s onwards, the Western system underwent some vital changes.[1] There was a shift from traditional industrial manufacture to a "postindustrial" culture of consumerism, communications, information technology and the service industry. Small-scale, decentralised, versatile, nonhierarchical enterprises were the order of the day. Markets were deregulated, and the working-class movement subjected to savage legal and political assault. Traditional class allegiances were weakened, while local, gender and ethnic identities grew more insistent. Politics became increasingly managed and manipulated.

The new information technologies played a key role in the increasing globalisation of the system, as a handful of transnational corporations distributed production and investment across the planet in pursuit of the readiest profits. A good deal of manufacturing was outsourced to cheap wage locations in the "underdeveloped" world, leading some parochially minded Westerners to conclude that heavy industry had disappeared from the planet altogether. Massive international migrations of labour followed in the wake of this global mobility, and with them a resurgence of racism and fascism as impoverished immigrants poured into the more advanced economies. While "peripheral" countries were subject to sweated labour, privatized facilities, slashed welfare and surreally inequitable terms of trade, the bestubbled executives of the metropolitan nations tore off their ties, threw open their shirt necks and fretted about their employees' spiritual well-being.

TERRY EAGLETON

4

None of this happened because the capitalist system was in blithe, buoyant mood. On the contrary, its newly pugnacious posture, like most forms of aggression, sprang from deep anxiety. If the system became manic, it was because it was latently depressed. What drove this reorganisation above all was the sudden fade-out of the postwar boom. Intensified international competition was forcing down rates of profits, drying up sources of investment and slowing the rate of growth. Even social democracy was now too radical and expensive a political option. The stage was thus set for Reagan and Thatcher, who would help to dismantle traditional manufacture, shackle the labour movement, let the market rip, strengthen the repressive arm of the state and champion a new social philosophy known as barefaced greed. The displacement of investment from manufacture to the service, financial and communications industries was a reaction to a protracted economic crisis, not a leap out of a bad old world into a brave new one.

Even so, it is doubtful that most of the radicals who changed their minds about the system between the '70s and '80s did so simply because there were fewer cotton mills around. It was not this that led them to ditch Marxism along with their sideburns and headbands, but the growing conviction that the regime they confronted was simply too hard to crack. It was not illusions about the new capitalism, but disillusion about the possibility of changing it, which proved decisive. There were, to be sure, plenty of former socialists who rationalised their gloom by claiming that if the system could not be changed, neither did it need to be. But it was lack of faith in an alternative that proved conclusive. Because the working-class movement had been so battered and bloodied, and the political left so robustly rolled back, the future seemed to have vanished without trace. For some on the left, the fall of the Soviet bloc in the late 1980s served to deepen the disenchantment. It did not help that the most successful radical current of the modern age—revolutionary nationalism—was by this time pretty well exhausted. What bred the culture of postmodernism, with its dismissal of so-called grand narratives and triumphal announcement of the End of History, was above all the conviction that the future would now be simply more of the present. Or, as one exuberant postmodernist put it, "The present plus more options."

What helped to discredit Marxism above all, then, was a creeping sense of political impotence. It is hard to sustain your faith in change when change seems off the agenda, even if this is when you need to sustain it most of all. After all, if you do not resist the apparently inevitable, you will never know how inevitable the inevitable was. If the fainthearted had managed to cling to their former views for another two decades, they would have witnessed a capitalism so exultant and impregnable that in 2008 it only just managed to keep the cash machines open on the high streets. They would also have seen a whole continent south of the Panama Canal shift decisively to the political left. The End of History was now at an end. In any case, Marxists ought to be well accustomed to defeat. They had known greater catastrophes than this. The political odds will always be on the system in power, if only because it has more tanks than you do. But the heady visions and effervescent hopes of the late 1960s made this downturn an especially bitter pill for the survivors of that era to swallow.

What made Marxism seem implausible, then, was not that capitalism had changed its spots. The case was exactly the opposite. It was the fact that as far as the system went, it was business as usual but even more so. Ironically, then, what helped to beat back Marxism also lent a kind of credence to its claims. It was thrust to the margins because the social order it confronted, far from growing more moderate and benign, waxed more ruthless and extreme than it had been before. And this made the Marxist critique of it all the more pertinent. On a global scale, capital was more concentrated and predatory than ever, and the working class had actually increased in size. It was becoming possible to imagine a future in which the megarich took shelter in their armed and gated communities, while a billion or so slum dwellers were encircled in their fetid hovels by watchtowers and barbed wire. In these circumstances, to claim that Marxism was finished was rather like claiming that firefighting was out of date because arsonists were growing more crafty and resourceful than ever.

In our own time, as Marx predicted, inequalities of wealth have dramatically deepened. The income of a single Mexican billionaire today is equivalent to the earnings of the poorest seventeen million of his compatriots. Capitalism has created more prosperity than history has ever witnessed, but the cost— not least in the near-destitution of billions—has been astronomical. According to the World Bank, 2.74 billion people in 2001 lived on less than two dollars a day. We face a probable future of nuclear-armed states warring over a scarcity of resources; and that scarcity is largely the consequence of capitalism itself. For the first time in history, our prevailing form of life has the power not simply to breed racism and spread cultural cretinism, drive us into war or herd us into labour camps, but to wipe us from the planet. Capitalism will behave antisocially if it is profitable for it to do so, and that can now mean human devastation on an unimaginable scale. What used to be apocalyptic fantasy is today no more than sober realism. The traditional leftist slogan "Socialism or barbarism" was never more grimly apposite, never less of a mere rhetorical flourish. In these dire conditions, as Fredric Jameson writes, "Marxism must necessarily become true again."[2]

Spectacular inequalities of wealth and power, imperial warfare, intensified exploitation, an increasingly repressive state: if all these characterize today's world, they are also the issues on which Marxism has acted and reflected for almost two centuries. One would expect, then, that it might have a few lessons to teach the present. Marx himself was particularly struck by the extraordinarily violent process by which an urban working class had been forged out of an uprooted peasantry in his own adopted country of England—a process which Brazil, China, Russia and India are living through today. Tristram Hunt points out that Mike Davis's book *Planet of Slums,* which documents the "stinking mountains of shit" known as slums to be found in the Lagos or Dhaka of today, can be seen as an updated version of Engels's *The Condition of the Working Class.* As China becomes the workshop of the world, Hunt comments, "the special economic zones of Guangdong and Shanghai appear eerily reminiscent of 1840s Manchester and Glasgow."[3]

What if it were not Marxism that is outdated but capitalism itself? Back in Victorian England, Marx saw the system as having already run out of steam. Having promoted social development in its heyday, it was now acting as a drag on it. He viewed capitalist society as awash with fantasy and fetishism, myth and idolatry, however much it prided itself on its modernity. Its very enlightenment—its smug belief in its own superior rationality—was a kind of superstition. If it was capable of some astonishing progress, there was another sense in which it had to run very hard just to stay on the spot. The final limit on capitalism, Marx once commented, is capital itself, the constant reproduction of which is a frontier beyond which it cannot stray. There is thus something curiously static and repetitive about this most dynamic of all historical regimes. The fact that its underlying logic remains pretty constant is one reason why the Marxist critique of it remains largely valid. Only if the system were genuinely able to break beyond its own bounds, inaugurating something unimaginably new, would this cease to be the case. But capitalism is incapable of inventing a future which does not ritually reproduce its present. With, needless to say, more options . . .

Capitalism has brought about great material advances. But though this way of organising our affairs has had a long time to demonstrate that it is capable of satisfying human demands all round, it seems no closer to doing so than ever. How long are we prepared to wait for it to come up with the goods? Why do we continue to indulge the myth that the fabulous wealth generated by this mode of production will in the fullness of time become available to all? Would the world treat similar claims by the far left with such genial, let's-wait-and-see forbearance? Right-wingers who concede that there will always be colossal injustices in the system, but that that's just tough and the alternatives are even worse, are at least more honest in their hard-faced way than those who preach that it will all finally come right. If there happened to be both rich and poor people, as there happen to be both black and white ones, then the advantages of the well-heeled might well spread in time to the hard-up. But to point out that some people are destitute while others are prosperous is rather like claiming that the world contains both detectives and criminals. So it does; but this obscures the truth that there are detectives *because* there are criminals . . .

TWO

Marxism may be all very well in theory. Whenever it has been put into practice, however, the result has been terror, tyranny and mass murder on an inconceivable scale. Marxism might look like a good idea to well-heeled Western academics who can take freedom and democracy for granted. For millions of ordinary men and women, it has meant famine, hardship, torture, forced labour, a broken economy and a monstrously oppressive state. Those who continue to support the theory despite all this are either obtuse, self-deceived or morally contemptible. Socialism means lack of freedom; it also means a lack of material goods, since this is bound to be the result of abolishing markets.

Lots of men and women in the West are fervent supporters of bloodstained setups. Christians, for example. Nor is it unknown for decent, compassionate types to support whole civilisations steeped in blood. Liberals and conservatives, among others. Modern capitalist nations are the fruit of a history of slavery, genocide, violence and exploitation every bit as abhorrent as Mao's China or Stalin's Soviet Union. Capitalism, too, was forged in blood and tears; it is just that it has survived long enough to forget about much of this horror, which is not the case with Stalinism and Maoism. If Marx was spared this amnesia, it was partly because he lived while the system was still in the making.

Mike Davis writes in his *Late Victorian Holocausts* of the tens of millions of Indians, Africans, Chinese, Brazilians, Koreans, Russians and others who died as a result of entirely preventable famine, drought and disease in the late nineteenth century. Many of these catastrophes were the result of free market dogma, as (for example) soaring grain prices thrust food beyond the reach of the common people. Nor are all such monstrosities as old as the Victorians. During the last two decades of the twentieth century, the number of those in the world living on less than two dollars a day has increased by almost one hundred million.[1] One in three children in Britain today lives below the breadline, while bankers sulk if their annual bonus falls to a paltry million pounds.

Capitalism, to be sure, has bequeathed us some inestimably precious goods along with these abominations. Without the middle classes Marx so deeply admired, we would lack a heritage of liberty, democracy, civil rights, feminism, republicanism, scientific progress and a good deal more, as well as a history of slumps, sweatshops, fascism, imperial wars and Mel Gibson. But the so-called socialist system had its achievements, too. China and the Soviet Union dragged their citizens out of economic backwardness into the modern industrial world, at however horrific a human cost; and the cost was so steep partly because of the hostility of the capitalist West. That hostility also forced the Soviet Union into an arms race which crippled its arthritic economy even further, and finally pressed it to the point of collapse.

In the meantime, however, it managed along with its satellites to achieve cheap housing, fuel, transport and culture, full employment and impressive social services for half the citizens of Europe, as well as an incomparably greater degree of equality and (in the end) material well-being than those nations had previously enjoyed. Communist East Germany could boast of one of the finest child care systems in the world. The Soviet Union played a heroic role in combating the evil of fascism, as well as in helping to topple colonialist powers. It also fostered the kind of solidarity among its citizens that Western nations seem able to muster only when they are killing the natives of other lands. All this, to be sure, is no substitute for freedom, democracy and vegetables in the shop, but neither is it to be ignored. When freedom and democracy finally rode to the rescue of the Soviet bloc, they did so in the shape of economic shock therapy, a form of daylight robbery politely known as privatization, joblessness for tens of millions, stupendous increases in poverty and inequality, the closure of free nurseries, the loss of women's rights and the near-ruin of the social welfare networks that had served these countries so well.

Even so, the gains of Communism scarcely outweigh

the losses. It may be that some kind of dictatorial government was well-nigh inevitable in the atrocious conditions of the early Soviet Union; but this did not have to mean Stalinism, or anything like it. Taken overall, Maoism and Stalinism were botched, bloody experiments which made the very idea of socialism stink in the nostrils of many of those elsewhere in the world who had most to benefit from it. But what about capitalism? As I write, unemployment in the West is already in the millions and is mounting steadily higher, and capitalist economies have been prevented from imploding only by the appropriation of trillions of dollars from their hard-pressed citizens. The bankers and financiers who have brought the world financial system to the brink of the abyss are no doubt queuing up for cosmetic surgery, lest they are spotted and torn limb from limb by enraged citizens.

It is true that capitalism works some of the time, in the sense that it has brought untold prosperity to some sectors of the world. But it has done so, as did Stalin and Mao, at a staggering human cost. This is not only a matter of genocide, famine, imperialism and the slave trade. The system has also proved incapable of breeding affluence without creating huge swathes of deprivation alongside it. It is true that this may not matter much in the long run, since the capitalist way of life is now threatening to destroy the planet altogether. One eminent Western economist has described climate change as "the greatest market failure in history."[2]

Marx himself never imagined that socialism could be achieved in impoverished conditions. Such a project would require almost as bizarre a loop in time as inventing the Internet in the Middle Ages. Nor did any Marxist thinker until Stalin imagine that this was possible, including Lenin, Trotsky and the rest of the Bolshevik leadership. You cannot reorganise wealth for the benefit of all if there is precious little wealth to reorganise. You cannot abolish social classes in conditions of scarcity, since conflicts over a material surplus too meagre to meet everyone's needs will simply revive them again. As Marx comments in *The German Ideology,* the result of a revolution in such conditions is that "the old filthy business" (or in less tasteful translation, "the same old crap") will simply reappear. All you will get is socialised scarcity. If you need to accumulate capital more or less from scratch, then the most effective way of doing so, however brutal, is through the profit motive. Avid self-interest is likely to pile up wealth with remarkable speed, though it is likely to amass spectacular poverty at the same time.

Nor did Marxists ever imagine that it was possible to achieve socialism in one country alone. The movement was international or it was nothing. This was a hardheaded materialist claim, not a piously idealist one. If a socialist nation failed to win international support in a world where production was specialized and divided among different nations, it would be unable to draw upon the global resources needed to abolish scarcity. The productive wealth of a single country was unlikely to be enough. The outlandish notion of socialism in one country was invented by Stalin in the 1920s, partly as a cynical rationalisation of the fact that other nations had been unable to come to the aid of the Soviet Union. It has no warrant in Marx himself. Socialist revolutions must of course start somewhere. But they cannot be completed within national boundaries. To judge socialism by its results in one desperately isolated country would be like drawing conclusions about the human race from a study of psychopaths in Kalamazoo.

Building up an economy from very low levels is a backbreaking, dispiriting task. It is unlikely that men and women will freely submit to the hardships it involves. So unless this project is executed gradually, under democratic control and in accordance with socialist values, an authoritarian state may step in and force its citizens to do what they are reluctant to undertake voluntarily. The militarization of labour in Bolshevik Russia is a case in point. The result, in a grisly irony, will be to undermine the political superstructure of socialism (popular democracy, genuine self-government) in the very attempt to build up its economic base. It would be like being invited to a party only to discover that you had not only to bake the cakes and brew the beer but to dig the foundations and lay the floorboards. There wouldn't be much time to enjoy yourself.

Why Marx Was Right

Ideally, socialism requires a skilled, educated, politically sophisticated populace, thriving civic institutions, a well-evolved technology, enlightened liberal traditions and the habit of democracy. None of this is likely to be on hand if you cannot even afford to mend the dismally few highways you have, or have no insurance policy against sickness or starvation beyond a pig in the back shed. Nations with a history of colonial rule are especially likely to be bereft of the benefits I have just listed, since colonial powers have not been remarkable for their zeal to implant civil liberties or democratic institutions among their underlings.

As Marx insists, socialism also requires a shortening of the working day—partly to provide men and women with the leisure for personal fulfillment, partly to create time for the business of political and economic self-government. You cannot do this if people have no shoes; and to distribute shoes among millions of citizens is likely to require a centralised bureaucratic state. If your nation is under invasion from an array of hostile capitalist powers, as Russia was in the wake of the Bolshevik revolution, an autocratic state will seem all the more inevitable. Britain during the Second World War was far from an autocracy; but it was by no means a free country, and one would not have expected it to be.

To go socialist, then, you need to be reasonably well-heeled, in both the literal and metaphorical senses of the term. No Marxist from Marx and Engels to Lenin and Trotsky ever dreamt of anything else. Or if you are not well-heeled your-self, then a sympathetic neighbour reasonably flush in mate-rial resources needs to spring to your aid. In the case of the Bolsheviks, this would have meant such neighbours (Ger-many in particular) having their own revolutions, too. If the working classes of these countries could overthrow their own capitalist masters and lay hands on their productive powers, they could use those resources to save the first workers' state in history from sinking without trace. This was not as im-probable a proposal as it might sound. Europe at the time was aflame with revolutionary hopes, as councils of workers' and soldiers' deputies (or soviets) sprang up in cities such as Ber-lin, Warsaw, Vienna, Munich and Riga. Once these insurrec-tions were defeated, Lenin and Trotsky knew that their own revolution was in dire straits.

It is not that the building of socialism cannot be begun in deprived conditions. It is rather that without material re-sources it will tend to twist into the monstrous caricature of socialism known as Stalinism. The Bolshevik revolution soon found itself besieged by imperial Western armies, as well as threatened by counterrevolution, urban famine and a bloody civil war. It was marooned in an ocean of largely hostile peasants reluctant to hand over their hard-earned surplus at gunpoint to the starving towns. With a narrow capitalist base, disastrously low levels of material production, scant traces of civil institutions, a decimated, exhausted working class,

Why Marx Was Right

peasant revolts and a swollen bureaucracy to rival the Tsar's, the revolution was in deep trouble almost from the outset. In the end, the Bolsheviks were to march their starving, despondent, war-weary people into modernity at the point of a gun. Many of the most politically militant workers had perished in the Western-backed civil war, leaving the Bolshevik party with a dwindling social base. It was not long before the party usurped the workers' soviets and banned an independent press and justice system. It suppressed political dissent and oppositional parties, manipulated elections and militarized labour. This ruthlessly antisocialist programme came about against a background of civil war, widespread starvation and foreign invasion. Russia's economy lay in ruins, and its social fabric had disintegrated. In a tragic irony that was to mark the twentieth century as a whole, socialism proved least possible where it was most necessary.

The historian Isaac Deutscher depicts the situation with his usual matchless eloquence. The situation in Russia at the time "meant that the first and so far the only attempt to build socialism would have to be undertaken in the worst possible conditions, without the advantages of an intensive international division of labour, without the fertilizing influence of old and complex cultural traditions, in an environment of such staggering material and cultural poverty, primitiveness, and crudity as would tend to mar or warp the very striving for socialism."[3] It takes an unusually bold-faced critic of

Marxism to claim that none of this is relevant since Marxism is an authoritarian creed in any case. If it took over the Home Counties tomorrow, so the case goes, there would be labour camps in Dorking before the week was out.

Marx himself, as we shall see, was a critic of rigid dogma, military terror, political suppression and arbitrary state power. He believed that political representatives should be accountable to their electors, and castigated the German Social Democrats of his day for their statist politics. He insisted on free speech and civil liberties, was horrified by the forced creation of an urban proletariat (in his case in England rather than Russia), and held that common ownership in the countryside should be a voluntary rather than coercive process. Yet as one who recognized that socialism cannot thrive in poverty-stricken conditions, he would have understood perfectly how the Russian revolution came to be lost.

In fact, there is a paradoxical sense in which Stalinism, rather than discrediting Marx's work, bears witness to its validity. If you want a compelling account of how Stalinism comes about, you have to go to Marxism. Mere moral denunciations of the beast are simply not good enough. We need to know in what material conditions it arises, how it functions and how it might fail, and this knowledge has been best provided by certain mainstream currents of Marxism. Such Marxists, many of them followers of Leon Trotsky or of one or another "libertarian" brand of socialism, differ from

Western liberals in one vital respect: their criticisms of the so-called communist societies have been far more deep-seated. They have not contented themselves with wistful pleas for more democracy or civil rights. Instead, they have called for the overthrow of the entire repressive system, and called for this precisely as socialists. Moreover, they have been issuing such calls almost since the day that Stalin took power. At the same time, they have warned that if the communist system were to collapse, it might well be into the arms of a predatory capitalism waiting hungrily to pick among the ruins. Leon Trotsky foresaw precisely such an end to the Soviet Union, and was proved right some twenty years ago.

Imagine a slightly crazed capitalist outfit that tried to turn a premodern tribe into a set of ruthlessly acquisitive, technologically sophisticated entrepreneurs speaking the jargon of public relations and free market economics, all in a surreally short period of time. Does the fact that the experiment would almost certainly prove less than dramatically successful constitute a fair condemnation of capitalism? Surely not. To think so would be as absurd as claiming that the Girl Guides should be disbanded because they cannot solve certain tricky problems in quantum physics. Marxists do not believe that the mighty liberal lineage from Thomas Jefferson to John Stuart Mill is annulled by the existence of secret CIA-run prisons for torturing Muslims, even though such prisons are part of the politics of today's liberal societies. Yet the critics of Marxism are rarely willing to concede that show trials and mass terror are no refutation of it.

There is, however, another sense in which socialism is thought by some to be unworkable. Even if you were to build it under affluent conditions, how could you possibly run a complex modern economy without markets? The answer for a growing number of Marxists is that you do not need to. Markets in their view would remain an integral part of a socialist economy. So-called market socialism envisages a future in which the means of production would be socially owned, but where self-governing cooperatives would compete with one another in the marketplace.[4] In this way, some of the virtues of the market could be retained, while some of its vices could be shed. At the level of individual enterprises, cooperation would ensure increased efficiency, since the evidence suggests that it is almost always as efficient as capitalist enterprise and often much more so. At the level of the economy as a whole, competition ensures that the informational, allocation and incentive problems associated with the traditional Stalinist model of central planning do not arise.

Some Marxists claim that Marx himself was a market socialist, at least in the sense that he believed that the market would linger on during the transitional period following a socialist revolution. He also considered that markets had been emancipatory as well as exploitative, helping to free men and women from their previous dependence on lords and masters. Markets strip the aura of mystery from social relations, laying bare their bleak reality. So keen was Marx on this point that the philosopher Hannah Arendt once described the opening pages of the *Communist Manifesto* as "the greatest praise of capitalism you ever saw."[5] Market socialists also point out that markets are by no means specific to capitalism. Even Trotsky, so some of his disciples may be surprised to hear, supported the market, though only in the period of transition to socialism and in combination with economic planning. It was needed, he thought, as a check on the adequacy and rationality of planning, since "economic accounting is unthinkable without market relations."[6] Along with the Soviet Left Opposition, he was a strong critic of the so-called command economy.

Market socialism does away with private property, social classes and exploitation. It also places economic power into the hands of the actual producers. In all of these ways, it is a welcome advance on a capitalist economy. For some Marxists, however, it retains too many features of that economy to be palatable. Under market socialism there would still be commodity production, inequality, unemployment and the sway of market forces beyond human control. How would workers not simply be transformed into collective capitalists, maximizing their profits, cutting quality, ignoring social needs and pandering to consumerism in the drive for constant accumulation? How would one avoid the chronic short-termism of markets, their habit of ignoring the overall social picture and the long-term antisocial effects of their own fragmented decisions? Education and state monitoring might diminish these dangers, but some Marxists look instead to an economy which would be neither centrally planned nor market-governed.[7] On this model, resources would be allocated by negotiations between producers, consumers, environmentalists and other relevant parties, in networks of workplace, neighbourhood and consumer councils. The broad parameters of the economy, including decisions on the overall allocation of resources, rates of growth and investment, energy, transport and ecological policies and the like, would be set by representative assemblies at local, regional and national level. These general decisions about, say, allocation would then be devolved downwards to regional and local levels, where more detailed planning would be progressively worked out. At every stage, public debate over alternative economic plans and policies would be essential. In this way, what and how we produce could be determined by social need rather than private profit. Under capitalism, we are deprived of the power to decide whether we want to produce more hospitals or more breakfast cereals. Under socialism, this freedom would be regularly exercised.

Power in such assemblies would pass by democratic election from the bottom up rather than from the top down. Democratically elected bodies representing each branch of

Why Marx Was Right

commerce or production would negotiate with a national economic commission to achieve an agreed set of investment decisions. Prices would be determined not centrally, but by production units on the basis of input from consumers, users, interest groups and so on. Some champions of such so-called participatory economics accept a kind of mixed socialist economy: goods which are of vital concern to the community (food, health, pharmaceuticals, education, transport, energy, subsistence products, financial institutions, the media and the like) need to be brought under democratic public control, since those who run them tend to behave antisocially if they sniff the chance of enlarged profits in doing so. Less socially indispensable goods, however (consumer items, luxury products), could be left to the operations of the market. Some market socialists find this whole scheme too complex to be workable. As Oscar Wilde once remarked, the trouble with socialism is that it takes up too many evenings. Yet one needs at least to take account of the role of modern information technology in oiling the wheels of such a system. Even the former vice-president of Procter & Gamble has acknowledged that it makes workers' self-management a real possibility.[8] Besides, Pat Devine reminds us of just how much time is currently consumed by capitalist administration and organisation.[9] There is no obvious reason why the amount of time taken up by a socialist alternative should be greater.

Some advocates of the participatory model hold that

everyone should be remunerated equally for the same amount of work, despite differences of talent, training and occupation. As Michael Albert puts it, "The doctor working in a plush setting with comfortable and fulfilling circumstances earns more than the assembly worker working in a horrible din, risking life and limb, and enduring boredom and denigration, regardless of how long or how hard each works."[10] There is, in fact, a strong case for paying those who engage in boring, heavy, dirty or dangerous work more than, say, medics or academics whose labours are considerably more rewarding. Much of this dirty and dangerous work could perhaps be carried out by former members of the royal family. We need to reverse our priorities.

Since I have just mentioned the media as ripe for public ownership, let us take this as an exemplary case. Over half a century ago, in an excellent little book entitled *Communications,*[11] Raymond Williams outlined a socialist plan for the arts and media which rejected state control of its content on the one hand and the sovereignty of the profit motive on the other. Instead, the active contributors in this field would have control of their own means of expression and communication. The actual "plant" of the arts and media—radio stations, concert halls, TV networks, theatres, newspaper offices and so on—would be taken into public ownership (of which there are a variety of forms), and their management invested in democratically elected bodies. These would include both members of the public and representatives of media or artistic bodies.

These commissions, which would be strictly independent of the state, would then be responsible for awarding public resources and "leasing" the socially owned facilities either to individual practitioners or to independent, democratically self-governing companies of actors, journalists, musicians and the like. These men and women could then produce work free of both state regulation and the distorting pressures of the market. Among other things, we would be free of the situation in which a bunch of power-crazed, avaricious bullies dictate through their privately owned media outlets what the public should believe—which is to say, their own self-interested opinions and the system they support. We will know that socialism has established itself when we are able to look back with utter incredulity on the idea that a handful of commercial thugs were given free rein to corrupt the minds of the public with Neanderthal political views convenient for their own bank balances but for little else.

Much of the media under capitalism avoid difficult, controversial or innovative work because it is bad for profits. Instead, they settle for banality, sensationalism and gut prejudice. Socialist media, by contrast, would not ban everything but Schoenberg, Racine and endless dramatized versions of Marx's *Capital*. There would be popular theatre, TV and newspapers galore. "Popular" does not necessarily mean "inferior." Nelson Mandela is popular but not inferior. Plenty of ordinary people read highly specialist journals littered with jargon unintelligible to outsiders. It is just that these journals tend to be about angling, farm equipment or dog breeding rather than aesthetics or endocrinology. The popular becomes junk and kitsch when the media feel the need to hijack as large a slice of the market as quickly and painlessly as possible. And this need is for the most part commercially driven.

Socialists will no doubt continue to argue about the detail of a postcapitalist economy. There is no flawless model currently on offer. One can contrast this imperfection with the capitalist economy, which is in impeccable working order and which has never been responsible for the mildest touch of poverty, waste or slump. It has admittedly been responsible for some extravagant levels of unemployment, but the world's leading capitalist nation has hit on an ingenious solution to this defect. In the United States today, over a million more people would be seeking work if they were not in prison.

THREE

Marxism is a form of determinism. It sees men and women simply as the tools of history, and thus strips them of their freedom and individuality. Marx believed in certain iron laws of history, which work themselves out with inexorable force and which no human action can resist. Feudalism was fated to give birth to capitalism, and capitalism will inevitably give way to socialism. As such, Marx's theory of history is just a secular version of Providence or Destiny. It is offensive to human freedom and dignity, just as Marxist states are.

We may begin by asking what is distinctive about Marxism. What does Marxism have that no other political theory does? It is clearly not the idea of revolution, which long predates Marx's work. Nor is it the notion of communism, which is of ancient provenance. Marx did not invent socialism or communism. The working-class movement in Europe had already arrived at socialist ideas while Marx himself was still a liberal. In fact, it is hard to think of any single *political* feature that is unique to his thought. It is certainly not the idea of the revolutionary party, which comes to us from the French Revolution. Marx has precious little to say about it in any case.

What about the concept of social class? This won't do either, since Marx himself rightly denied that he invented the idea. It is true that he importantly redefined the whole concept, but it is not his own coinage. Nor did he think up the idea of the proletariat, which was familiar to a number of nineteenth-century thinkers. His idea of alienation was derived mostly from Hegel. It was also anticipated by the great Irish socialist and feminist, William Thompson. We shall also see later that Marx is not alone in giving such high priority to the economic in social life. He believes in a cooperative society free of exploitation run by the producers themselves, and holds that this could come about only by revolutionary means. But so did the great twentieth-century socialist Raymond Williams, who did not consider himself a Marxist. Plenty of anarchists, libertarian socialists and others would endorse this social vision but vehemently reject Marxism.

Two major doctrines lie at the heart of Marx's thought. One of them is the primary role played by the economic in social life; the other is the idea of a succession of modes of production throughout history. We shall see later, however, that neither of these notions was Marx's own innovation. Is what is peculiar to Marxism, then, the concept not of class but of class *struggle*? This is certainly close to the core of Marx's thought, but it is no more original to him than the idea of class itself. Take this couplet about a wealthy landlord from Oliver Goldsmith's poem "The Deserted Village":

> The robe that wraps his limbs in silken sloth
> Has robbed the neighbouring fields of half their
> growth.

The symmetry and economy of the lines themselves, with their neatly balanced antithesis, contrast with the waste and imbalance of the economy they describe. The couplet is clearly about class struggle. What robes the landlord robs his tenants. Or take these lines from John Milton's *Comus*:

> If every just man that now pines with want
> Had but a moderate and beseeming share
> Of that which lewdly pampered luxury
> Now heaps upon some few with vast excess,
> Nature's full blessings would be well dispensed
> In unsuperfluous even proportion . . .

Much the same sentiment is expressed by King Lear. In fact, Milton has quietly stolen this idea from Shakespeare. Voltaire believed that the rich grew bloated on the blood of the poor, and that property lay at the heart of social conflict. Jean-Jacques Rousseau, as we shall see, argued much the same. The idea of class struggle is by no means peculiar to Marx, as he himself was well aware.

Even so, it is mightily central to him. So central, in fact, that he sees it as nothing less than the force that drives human history. It is the very motor or dynamic of human development, which is not an idea that would have occurred to John Milton. Whereas many social thinkers have seen human society as an organic unity, what constitutes it in Marx's view is division. It is made up of mutually incompatible interests. Its logic is one of conflict rather than cohesion. For example, it is in the interest of the capitalist class to keep wages low, and in the interests of wage earners to push them higher.

Marx famously declares in the *Communist Manifesto* that "the history of all previously existing society is the history of class struggles." He can't of course mean this literally. If brushing my teeth last Wednesday counts as part of history, then it is hard to see that this is a matter of class struggle. Bowling a leg break in cricket or being pathologically obsessed with penguins is not burningly relevant to class struggle. Perhaps "history" refers to public events, not private ones like brushing one's teeth. But that brawl in the bar last night was public enough. So perhaps history is confined to *major* public events. But by whose definition? Anyway, how was the Great Fire of London a product of class struggle? It might count as an instance of class struggle if Che Guevara had been run over by a truck, but only if a CIA agent was at the wheel. Otherwise it would have just been an accident. The story of women's oppression interlocks with the history of class struggle, but it is not just an aspect of it. The same goes for the poetry of Wordsworth or Seamus Heaney. Class struggle can't cover everything.

Maybe Marx did not take his own claim literally. The *Communist Manifesto,* after all, is intended as a piece of political propaganda, and as such is full of rhetorical flour-ishes. Even so, there is an important question about how much Marxist thought does in fact include. Some Marxists seem to have treated it as a Theory of Everything, but this is surely not so. The fact that Marxism has nothing very inter-esting to say about malt whiskies or the nature of the uncon-scious, the haunting fragrance of a rose or why there is some-thing rather than nothing, is not to its discredit. It is not intended to be a total philosophy. It does not give us accounts of beauty or the erotic, or of how the poet Yeats achieves the curious resonance of his verse. It has been mostly silent on questions of love, death and the meaning of life. It has, to be sure, a very grand narrative to deliver, which stretches all the way from the dawning of civilisation to the present and fu-ture. But there are other grand narratives besides Marxism, such as the history of science or religion or sexuality, which interact with the story of class struggle but cannot be reduced to it. (Postmodernists tend to assume that there is either one grand narrative or just a lot of mini-narratives. But this is not the case.) So whatever Marx himself may have thought, "all history has been the history of class struggle" should not be taken to mean that everything that has ever happened is a matter of class struggle. It means, rather, that class struggle is what is most *fundamental* to human history.

Fundamental in what sense, though? How, for ex-ample, is it more fundamental than the history of religion, science or sexual oppression? Class is not necessarily fundamental in the sense of providing the strongest motive for political action. Think of the role of ethnic identity in that respect, to which Marxism has paid too little regard. Anthony Giddens claims that interstate conflicts, along with racial and sexual inequalities, "are of equal importance to class exploitation."[1] But equally important for what? Of equal moral and political importance, or equally important for the achievement of socialism? We sometimes call a thing fundamental if it is the necessary basis for something else; but it is hard to see that class struggle is the necessary basis of religious faith, scientific discovery or women's oppression, much involved with it though these things are. It does not seem true that if we kicked this foundation away, Buddhism, astrophysics and the Miss World contest would come tumbling down. They have relatively independent histories of their own.

So what *is* class struggle fundamental to? Marx's answer would seem to be twofold. It shapes a great many events, institutions and forms of thought which seem at first glance to be innocent of it; and it plays a decisive role in the turbulent transition from one epoch of history to another. By history, Marx means not "everything that has ever happened," but a specific trajectory underlying it. He is using "history" in the sense of the significant *course* of events, not as a synonym for the whole of human existence to date.

Why Marx Was Right

So is the idea of class struggle what distinguishes Marx's thought from other social theories? Not quite. We have seen that this notion is not original to him, any more than the concept of a mode of production is. What *is* unique about his thought is that he locks these two ideas—class struggle and mode of production—together, to provide a historical scenario which is indeed genuinely new. Quite how the two ideas go together has been a subject of debate among Marxists, and Marx himself hardly waxes eloquent on the point. But if we are in search of what is peculiar to his work, we could do worse than call a halt here. In essence, Marxism is a theory and practice of long-term historical change. The trouble, as we shall see, is that what is most peculiar to Marxism is also what is most problematic.

Broadly speaking, a mode of production for Marx means the combination of certain forces of production with certain relations of production. A force of production means any instrument by which we go to work on the world in order to reproduce our material life. The idea covers everything that promotes human mastery or control over Nature for productive purposes. Computers are a productive force if they play a part in material production as a whole, rather than just being used for chatting to serial killers disguised as friendly strangers. Donkeys in nineteenth-century Ireland were a productive force. Human labour power is a productive force. But these forces never exist in the raw. They are always bound up with certain social relations, by which Marx means relations between social classes. One social class, for example, may own and control the means of production, while another may find itself exploited by it.

Marx believes that the productive forces have a tendency to develop as history unfolds. This is not to claim that they progress all the time, since he also seems to hold that they can lapse into long periods of stagnation. The agent of this development is whatever social class is in command of material production. On this version of history, it is as though the productive forces "select" the class most capable of expanding them. There comes a point, however, when the prevailing social relations, far from promoting the growth of the productive forces, begin to act as an obstacle to them. The two run headlong into contradiction, and the stage is set for political revolution. The class struggle sharpens, and a social class capable of taking the forces of production forward assumes power from its erstwhile masters. Capitalism, for example, staggers from crisis to crisis, slump to slump, by virtue of the social relations it involves; and at a certain point in its decline, the working class is on hand to take over the ownership and control of production. At one point in his work, Marx even claims that no new social class takes over until the productive forces have been developed as far as possible by the previous one.

The case is put most succinctly in the following well-known passage:

> At a certain stage of their development, the material productive forces of society enter into contradiction with the existing relations of production, or—what is but a legal expression of the same thing—with the property relations within which they have been at work hitherto. From forms of development of the productive forces, these relations turn into their fetters. Then begins an epoch of social revolution.[2]

There are numerous problems with this theory, as Marxists themselves have been quick to point out. For one thing, why does Marx assume that by and large the productive forces keep evolving? It is true that technological development tends to be cumulative, in the sense that human beings are reluctant to let go of what advances they make in prosperity and efficiency. This is because as a species we are somewhat rational but also mildly indolent, and thus inclined to be labour-saving. (It is these factors which determine that supermarket checkout queues are always roughly the same length.) Having invented e-mail, we are unlikely to revert to scratching on rocks. We also have the ability to transmit such advances to future generations. Technological knowledge is rarely lost, even if the technology itself is destroyed. But this is so broad a truth that it does not serve to illuminate very much. It does not explain, for example, why the forces of production evolve very rapidly at certain times but may stagnate for centuries at others. Whether or not there is major technological development depends on the prevailing social relations, not on some built-in drive. Some Marxists see the compulsion to improve the forces of production not as a general law of history, but as an imperative specific to capitalism. They take issue with the assumption that every mode of production must be followed by a more productive one. Whether these Marxists include Marx himself is a contestable point.

For another thing, it is not clear by what mechanism certain social classes are "selected" for the task of promoting the productive forces. Those forces, after all, are not some ghostly personage able to survey the social scene and summon a particular candidate to their aid. Ruling classes do not of course promote the productive forces out of altruism, any more than they seize power for the express purpose of feeding the hungry and clothing the naked. Instead, they tend to pursue their own material interests, reaping a surplus from the labour of others. The idea, however, is that in doing so they unwittingly advance the productive forces as a whole, and along with them (at least in the long run) the spiritual as well as material wealth of humanity. They foster resources from which the majority in class-society are shut out, but in doing so build up a legacy that men and women as a whole will one day inherit in the communist future.

Marx clearly thinks that material wealth can damage our moral health. Even so, he does not see a gulf between the moral and the material, as some idealist thinkers do. In his view, the unfurling of the productive forces involves the unfolding of creative human powers and capacities. In one sense, history is not at all a tale of progress. Instead, we lurch from one form of class-society, one kind of oppression and exploitation, to another. In another sense, however, this grim narrative can be seen as a movement onwards and upwards, as human beings acquire more complex needs and desires, cooperate in more intricate, rewarding ways, and create new kinds of relationship and fresh sorts of fulfillment.

Human beings as a whole will come into this inheritance in the communist future; but the process of building it up is inseparable from violence and exploitation. In the end, social relations will be established that deploy this accumulated wealth for the benefit of all. But the process of accumulation itself involves excluding the great majority of men and women from enjoying its fruits. So it is, Marx comments, that history "progresses by its bad side." It looks as though injustice now is unavoidable for justice later. The end is at odds with the means: if there were no exploitation there would be no sizeable expansion of the productive forces, and if there were no such expansion there would be no material basis for socialism.

Marx is surely right to see that the material and spiritual are in both conflict and collusion. He does not simply damn class-society for its moral atrocities, though he does that too; he also recognizes that spiritual fulfillment requires a material foundation. You cannot have a decent relationship if you are starving. Every extension of human communication brings with it new forms of community and fresh kinds of division. New technologies may thwart human potential, but they can also enhance it. Modernity is not to be mindlessly celebrated, but neither is it to be disdainfully dismissed. Its positive and negative qualities are for the most part aspects of the same process. This is why only a dialectical approach, one which grasps how contradiction is of its essence, can do it justice.

All the same, there are real problems with Marx's theory of history. Why, for example, does the same mechanism—the conflict between the forces and relations of production—operate in the shift from one era of class-society to another? What accounts for this odd consistency over vast stretches of historical time? Anyway, is it not possible to overthrow a dominant class while it is still in its prime, if the political opposition is powerful enough? Do we really have to wait until the productive forces falter? And might not the growth of the productive forces actually undermine the class poised to take over—say, by fashioning new forms of oppressive technology? It is true that with the growth of the productive forces, workers tend to become more skilled, well-organised, educated and (perhaps) politically self-assured and sophisticated; but for the same reason there may also be more tanks, surveillance cameras, right-wing newspapers and modes of outsourcing labour around. New technologies may force more people into unemployment, and thus into political inertia. In any case, whether a social class is ripe to make a revolution is shaped by a lot more than whether it has the power to promote the forces of production. Class capacities are moulded by a whole range of factors. And how can we know that a specific set of social relations will be useful for that purpose?

A change of social relations cannot simply be explained by an expansion of the productive forces. Nor do pathbreaking changes in the productive forces necessarily result in new social relations, as the Industrial Revolution might illustrate. The same productive forces can coexist with different sets of social relations. Stalinism and industrial capitalism, for example. When it comes to peasant agriculture from ancient times to the modern age, a wide range of social relations and forms of property has proved possible. Or the same set of social relations might foster different kinds of productive forces. Think of capitalist industry and capitalist agriculture. Productive forces and productive relations do not dance harmoniously hand in hand throughout history. The truth is that each stage of development of the productive forces opens up a whole range of possible social relations, and there is no guarantee that any one set of them will actually come about. Neither is there any guarantee that a potential revolutionary agent will be conveniently on hand when the historical crunch comes. Sometimes there is simply no class around that could take the productive forces further, as happened in the case of classical China.

Even so, the connection between forces and relations is an illuminating one. Among other things, it allows us to recognize that you can only have certain social relations if the productive forces have evolved to a certain extent. If some people are to live a lot more comfortably than others, you need to produce a sizeable economic surplus; and this is possible only at a certain point of productive development. You cannot sustain an immense royal court complete with minstrels, pages, jesters and chamberlains if everyone has to herd goats or grub for plants all the time just to survive.

The class struggle is essentially a struggle over the surplus, and as such is likely to continue as long as there is not a sufficiency for all. Class comes about whenever material production is so organised as to compel some individuals to transfer their surplus labour to others in order to survive. When there is little or no surplus, as in so-called primitive communism, everyone has to work, nobody can live off the toil of others, so there can be no classes. Later, there is enough of a surplus to fund classes like feudal lords, who live by the labour of their underlings. Only with capitalism can enough surplus be generated for the abolition of scarcity, and thus of social classes, to become possible. But only socialism can put this into practice.

It is not clear, however, why the productive forces should always triumph over the social relations—why the latter seem so humbly deferential to the former. Besides, the theory does not seem to accord with the way that Marx actually portrays the transition from feudalism to capitalism, or in some respects from slavery to feudalism. It is also true that the same social classes have often persisted in power for centuries despite their inability to promote productive growth.

One of the obvious flaws of that model is its determinism. Nothing seems able to resist the onward march of the productive forces. History works itself out by an inevitable internal logic. There is a single "subject" of history (the constantly growing productive forces) which stretches all the way through it, throwing up different political setups as it rolls along. This is a metaphysical vision with a vengeance. Yet it is not a simpleminded scenario of Progress. In the end, the human powers and capacities which evolve along with the productive forces make for a finer kind of humanity. But the price we pay for this is a horrifying one. Every advance of the productive forces is a victory for both civilisation and barbarism. If it brings in its wake new possibilities of emancipation, it also arrives coated in blood. Marx was no naïve progress-monger. He was well aware of the terrible cost of communism.

It is true there is also class struggle, which would seem to suggest that men and women are free. It is hard to see that strikes, lockouts and occupations are dictated by some providential force. But what if this very freedom was, so to speak, preprogrammed, already factored into the unstoppable march of history? There is an analogy here with the Christian interplay between divine providence and human free will. For the Christian, I act freely when I strangle the local police chief; but God has foreseen this action from all eternity, and included it all along in his plan for humanity. He did not force me to dress up as a parlour maid last Friday and call myself Milly; but being omniscient, he knew that I would, and could thus shape his cosmic schemes with the Milly business well in mind. When I pray to him for a smarter-looking teddy bear than the dog-eared, beer-stained one who sleeps on my pillow at present, it is not that God never had the slightest intention of bestowing such a favour on me but then, on hearing my prayer, changed his mind. God cannot change his mind. It is rather that he decides from all eternity to give me a new teddy bear because of my prayer, which he has also foreseen from all eternity. In one sense, the coming of the future kingdom of God is not preordained: it will arrive only if men and women work for it in the present. But the fact that they will work for it of their own free will is itself an inevitable result of God's grace.

There is a similar interplay between freedom and inevitability in Marx. He sometimes seems to think that class struggle, though in one sense free, is bound to intensify under certain historical conditions, and that at times its outcome can be predicted with certainty. Take, for example, the question of socialism. Marx appears to regard the advent of socialism as inevitable. He says so more than once. In the *Communist Manifesto,* the fall of the capitalist class and the victory of the working class are described as "equally inevitable." But this is not because Marx believes that there is some secret law inscribed in history which will usher in socialism whatever men and women may or may not do. If this were so, why should he urge the need for political struggle? If socialism really is inevitable, one might think that we need do no more than wait for it to arrive, perhaps ordering curries or collecting tattoos in the meanwhile. Historical determinism is a recipe for political quietism. In the twentieth century, it played a key role in the failure of the communist movement to combat fascism, assured as it was for a time that fascism was no more than the death rattle of a capitalist system on the point of extinction. One might claim that whereas for the nineteenth century the inevitable was sometimes eagerly expected, this is not the case for us. Sentences beginning "It is now inevitable that . . ." generally have an ominous ring to them.

Marx does not think that the inevitability of socialism means we can all stay in bed. He believes, rather, that once capitalism has definitively failed, working people will have no reason not to take it over and every reason to do so. They will recognize that it is in their interests to change the system, and that, being a majority, they also have the power to do so. So they will act as the rational animals they are and establish an alternative. Why on earth would you drag out a wretched existence under a regime you are capable of changing to your advantage? Why would you let your foot itch intolerably when you are able to scratch it? Just as for the Christian human action is free yet part of a preordained plan, so for Marx the disintegration of capitalism will unavoidably lead men and women to sweep it away of their own free will.

He is talking, then, about what free men and women are bound to do under certain circumstances. But this is surely a contradiction, since freedom means that there is nothing that you are bound to do. You are not bound to devour a succulent pork chop if your guts are being wrenched by agonizing hunger pains. As a devout Muslim, you might prefer to die. If there is only one course of action I can possibly take, and if it is impossible for me not to take it, then in that situation I am not free. Capitalism may be teetering on the verge of ruin, but it may not be socialism that replaces it.

Why Marx Was Right

It may be fascism, or barbarism. Perhaps the working class will be too enfeebled and demoralized by the crumbling of the system to act constructively. In an uncharacteristically gloomy moment, Marx reflects that the class struggle may result in the "common ruination" of the contending classes.

Or—a possibility that he could not fully anticipate—the system might fend off political insurrection by reform. Social democracy is one bulwark between itself and disaster. In this way, the surplus reaped from developed productive forces can be used to buy off revolution, which does not fit at all neatly into Marx's historical scheme. He seems to have believed that capitalist prosperity can only be temporary; that the system will eventually founder; and that the working class will then inevitably rise up and take it over. But this, for one thing, passes over the many ways (much more sophisticated in our own day than in Marx's) in which even a capitalism in crisis can continue to secure the consent of its citizens. Marx did not have Fox News and the *Daily Mail* to reckon with.

There is, of course, another future one can envisage, namely no future at all. Marx could not foresee the possibility of nuclear holocaust or ecological catastrophe. Or perhaps the ruling class will be brought low by being hit by an asteroid, a fate that some of them might regard as preferable to socialist revolution. Even the most deterministic theory of history can be shipwrecked by such contingent events. All the same, we can still inquire how much of a historical determinist Marx actually is. If there were no more to his work than the idea of the productive forces giving birth to certain social relations, the answer would be plain. This amounts to a full-blown determinism, and as such a case that very few Marxists today would be prepared to sign up for.[3] On this view, it is not human beings who create their own history; it is the productive forces, which lead a strange, fetishistic life of their own.

Yet there is a different current of thought in Marx's writings, for which it is the social relations of production which have priority over the productive forces, rather than the other way around. If feudalism made way for capitalism, it was not because the latter could promote the productive forces more efficiently; it was because feudal social relations in the countryside were gradually ousted by capitalist ones. Feudalism created the conditions in which the new bourgeois class could grow up; but this class did not emerge as a result of a growth in the productive forces. Besides, if the forces of production expanded under feudalism, it was not because they have some built-in tendency to develop, but for reasons of class interest. As for the modern period, if the productive forces have grown so rapidly over the past couple of centuries, it is because capitalism cannot survive without constant expansion.

On this alternative theory, human beings, in the shape of social relations and class struggles, are indeed the authors of their own history. Marx once commented that he and

Engels had emphasized "the class struggle as the immediate driving force of history" for some forty years.[4] The point about class struggle is that its outcome cannot be predicted, and determinism can therefore find no foothold. You might always argue that class *conflict* is determined—that it is in the nature of social classes to pursue mutually clashing interests, and that this is determined by the mode of production. But it is only now and then that this "objective" conflict of interests takes the form of a full-scale political battle; and it is hard to see how that battle can be somehow predrafted. Marx may have thought that socialism was inevitable, but he surely did not think that the Factory Acts or the Paris Commune were. If he had really been a full-blooded determinist, he might have been able to tell us when and how socialism would arrive. But he was a prophet in the sense of denouncing injustice, not in the sense of peering into a crystal ball.

"History," Marx writes, "does nothing, it possesses no immense wealth, it wages no battles. It is man, real living man, who does all that, who possesses and fights; 'history' is not, as it were, a person apart, using man as a means to achieve its own aims, history is nothing but the activity of man pursuing his aims."[5] When Marx comments on class relations in the ancient, medieval or modern world, he often writes as though these are what are primary. He also insists that each mode of production, from slavery and feudalism to capitalism, has its own distinct laws of development. If this is so, then one no longer need think in terms of a rigorously "linear" historical process, in which each mode of production follows on the heels of another according to some inner logic. There is nothing endemic in feudalism that turns it inexorably into capitalism. There is no longer a single thread running through the tapestry of history, but rather a set of differences and discontinuities. It is bourgeois political economy, not Marxism, that thinks in terms of universal evolutionary laws. Indeed, Marx himself protested against the charge that he was seeking to bring the whole of history under a single law. He was deeply averse to such bloodless abstractions, as befits a good Romantic. "The materialist method turns into its opposite," he insisted, "if it is taken not as one's guiding principle of investigation but as a ready-made pattern to which one shapes the facts of history to suit oneself."[6] His view of the origins of capitalism, he warns, should not be transformed "into an historico-philosophical theory of the general path prescribed by fate to all nations whatever the historical circumstances in which they find themselves."[7] If there were certain tendencies at work in history, there were also countertendencies, which implies that outcomes are not assured.

Some Marxists have played down the "primacy of the productive forces" case, and played up the alternative theory we have just examined. But this is probably too defensive. The former model crops up in enough important spots in

Marx's work to suggest that he took it very seriously. It does not sound like a momentary aberration. It is also the way that Marxists like Lenin and Trotsky generally interpreted him. Some commentators claim that by the time he came to write *Capital,* Marx had more or less abandoned his previous faith in the productive forces as the heroes of history. Others are not so convinced. Students of Marx, however, are free to select whatever ideas in his work seem most plausible. Only Marxist fundamentalists regard that work as holy writ, and there are far fewer of those nowadays than the Christian variety.

There is no evidence that Marx is in general a determinist, in the sense of denying that human actions are free. On the contrary, he clearly believes in freedom, and talks all the time, not least in his journalism, about how individuals could (and sometimes should) have acted differently, whatever the historical limits placed on their choices. Engels, who some see as an out-and-out determinist, had a lifelong interest in military strategy, which is hardly a question of fate.[8] Marx is to be found stressing courage and consistency as essential for political victory, and seems to allow for the decisive influence of random events on historical processes. The fact that the militant working class in France was ravaged by cholera in 1849 is one such example.

There are, in any case, different kinds of inevitability. You may consider that some things are inevitable without being a determinist. Even libertarians believe that death is unavoidable. If enough Texans try to cram themselves into a telephone box, some of them will end up being seriously squashed. This is a matter of physics rather than fate. It does not alter the fact that they crammed themselves in of their own free will. Actions we freely perform often end up confronting us as alien powers. Marx's theories of alienation and commodity fetishism are based on just this truth.

There are other senses of inevitability as well. To claim that the triumph of justice in Zimbabwe is inevitable may not mean that it is bound to happen. It may be more of a moral or political imperative, meaning that the alternative is too dreadful to contemplate. "Socialism or barbarism" may not suggest that we will undoubtedly end up living under one or the other. It may be a way of emphasizing the unthinkable consequences of not achieving the former. Marx argues in *The German Ideology* that "at the present time . . . individuals *must* abolish private property," but that "*must*" is more of a political exhortation than a suggestion that they have no choice. Marx, then, may not be a determinist in general; but there are a good many formulations in his work which convey a sense of *historical* determinism. He sometimes compares historical laws to natural ones, writing in *Capital* of the "natural laws of capitalism . . . working with iron necessity towards inevitable results."[9] When a commentator describes his work as treating the evolution of society like a process of natural history, Marx seems to concur. He also approvingly quotes a reviewer of his work who sees it as demonstrating "the necessity of the present order of things, and the necessity of another order into which the first must inevitably pass."[10] It is not clear how this austere determinism fits with the centrality of class struggle.

There are times when Engels sharply distinguishes historical laws from natural ones, and other times when he argues for affinities between the two. Marx flirts with the idea of finding a basis for history in Nature, but also highlights the fact that we make the former but not the latter. Sometimes he criticizes the application of biology to human history, and rejects the notion of universally valid historical laws. Like many a nineteenth-century thinker, Marx hijacked the authority of the natural sciences, then the supreme model of knowledge, to gain some legitimacy for his work. But he might also have believed that so-called historical laws could be known with the certainty of scientific ones.

Even so, it is hard to credit that that he considered the so-called tendency of the rate of capitalist profit to decline as being literally like the law of gravity. He cannot have thought that history evolves as a thunderstorm does. It is true that he sees the course of historical events as revealing a significant shape, but he is hardly alone in holding that. Not many people see human history as completely random. If there were no regularities or broadly predictable tendencies in social life, we would be incapable of purposive action. It is not a choice between iron laws on the one hand and sheer chaos on the other. Every society, like every human action, opens up certain possible futures while shutting down others. But this interplay of freedom and constraint is far from some kind of cast-iron necessity. If you attempt to build socialism in wretched economic conditions, then as we have seen you are very likely to end up with some species of Stalinism. This is a well-testified historical pattern, confirmed by a whole number of bungled social experiments. Liberals and conservatives who do not usually relish talk of historical laws might change their tune when it comes to this particular instance of them. But to claim that you are *bound* to end up with Stalinism is to overlook the contingencies of history. Perhaps the common people will rise up and take power into their own hands; or perhaps a set of affluent nations will unexpectedly fly to your aid; or perhaps you might discover that you are sitting on the largest oil field on the planet and use this to build up your economy in a democratic way.

It is much the same with the course of history. Marx does not seem to believe that the various modes of production from ancient slavery to modern capitalism follow upon one another in some unalterable pattern. Engels remarked that history "moves often in leaps and bounds and in a zigzag line."[11] For one thing, different modes of production do not just follow each other in the first place. They can coexist within the same society. For another thing, Marx claimed that his views on the transition from feudalism to capitalism applied specifically to the West and were not to be universalised. As far as modes of production go, not every nation has to make the same trek from one to the other. The Bolsheviks were able to leap from a part-feudalist Russia to a socialist state without living through a prolonged interlude of extensive capitalism.

Marx believed at one point that his own nation of Germany had to pass through a stage of bourgeois rule before the working class could come to power. Later, however, he seems to have abandoned this belief, recommending instead a "permanent revolution" which would telescope these stages together. The typical Enlightenment view of history is of an organically evolving process, in which each phase emerges spontaneously from the next to constitute the whole we know as Progress. The Marxist narrative, by contrast, is marked by violence, disruption, conflict and discontinuity. There is indeed progress; but as Marx commented in his writings on India, it is like a hideous god who drinks nectar from the skulls of the slain.

How far Marx believes in historical necessity is not only a political and economic matter; it is also a moral one. He does not seem to suppose that feudalism or capitalism *had* to arise. Given a particular mode of production, there are various possible routes out of it. There are, of course, limits to this latitude. You would not move from consumer capitalism to hunter-gathering, unless perhaps a nuclear war had intervened in the meanwhile. Developed productive forces would make such a reversion both wholly unnecessary and deeply undesirable. But there is one move in particular which Marx seems to see as inevitable. This is the need for capitalism in order to have socialism. Driven by self-interest, ruthless competition and the need for ceaseless expansion, only capitalism is capable of developing the productive forces to the point where, under a different political dispensation, the surplus they generate can be used to furnish a sufficiency for all. To have socialism, you must first have capitalism. Or rather, *you* may not need to have capitalism, but *somebody* must. Marx thought that Russia might be able to achieve a form of socialism based on the peasant commune rather than on a history of industrial capitalism; but he did not imagine that this could be accomplished without the help of capitalist resources from elsewhere. A particular nation does not need to have passed through capitalism, but capitalism must exist somewhere or other if it is to go socialist.

This raises some thorny moral problems. Just as some Christians accept evil as somehow necessary to God's plan for humanity, so you can read Marx as claiming that capitalism, however rapacious and unjust, has to be endured for the sake of the socialist future it will inevitably bring in its wake. Not only endured, in fact, but actively encouraged. There are points in Marx's work where he cheers on the growth of capitalism, since only thus will the path to socialism be thrown open. In a lecture of 1847, for example, he defends free trade as hastening the advent of socialism. He also wanted to see German unification on the grounds that it would promote German capitalism. There are several places in his work where this revolutionary socialist betrays rather too much relish at the prospect of a progressive capitalist class putting paid to "barbarism."

The morality of this appears distinctly dubious. How is it different from Stalin's or Mao's murderous pogroms, executed in the name of the socialist future? How far does the end justify the means? And given that few today believe that socialism is inevitable, is this not even more reason for renouncing such a brutal sacrifice of the present on the altar of a future that might never arrive? If capitalism is essential for socialism, and if capitalism is unjust, does this not suggest that injustice is morally acceptable? If there is to be justice in the future, must there have been injustice in the past? Marx writes in *Theories of Surplus Value* that "the development of the capacities of the *human species* takes place at the cost of the majority of individuals and even classes."[12] He means that the good of the species will finally triumph in the shape of communism, but that this involves a great deal of ineluctable suffering and injustice en route. The material prosperity that in the end will fund freedom is the fruit of un-freedom.

There is a difference between doing evil in the hope that good may come of it, and seeking to turn someone else's evil to good use. Socialists did not perpetrate capitalism, and are innocent of its crimes; but granted that it exists, it seems rational to make the best of it. This is possible because capitalism is not of course simply evil. To think so is to be drastically one-sided, a fault by which Marx himself was rarely afflicted. As we have seen, the system breeds freedom as well as barbarism, emancipation along with enslavement. Capitalist society generates enormous wealth, but in a way that cannot help putting it beyond the reach of most of its citizens. Even so, that wealth can always be brought within reach. It can be disentangled from the acquisitive, individualist forms which bred it, invested in the community as a whole, and used to restrict disagreeable work to the minimum. It can thus release men and women from the chains of economic necessity into a life where they are free to realize their creative potential. This is Marx's vision of communism.

None of this suggests that the rise of capitalism was an absolute good. It would have been better if human emancipation could have been achieved with far less blood, sweat and tears. In this sense, Marx's theory of history is not a "teleological" one. A teleological theory holds that each phase of history arises inexorably from what went before. Each stage of the process is necessary in itself, and along with all the other stages is indispensable for attaining a certain goal. That goal is itself inevitable, and acts as the hidden dynamic of the whole process. Nothing in this narrative can be left out, and everything, however apparently noxious or negative, contributes to the good of the whole.

This is not what Marxism teaches. To say that capitalism can be drawn on for an improved future is not to imply that it exists for that reason. Nor does socialism follow necessarily from it. It is not to suggest that the crimes of capitalism are justified by the advent of socialism. Nor is it to clam that capitalism was bound to emerge. Modes of production do not arise necessarily. It is not as though they are linked to all previous stages by some inner logic. No stage of the process exists for the sake of the others. It is possible to leap stages, as with the Bolsheviks. And the end is by no means guaranteed. History for Marx is not moving in any particular direction. Capitalism can be used to build socialism, but there is no sense in which the whole historical process is secretly labouring towards this goal.

The modern capitalist age, then, brings its undoubted benefits. It has a great many features, from anaesthetics and penal reform to efficient sanitation and freedom of expression, which are precious in themselves, not simply because a socialist future might find some way to make use of them. But this does not necessarily mean that the system is finally vindicated. It is possible to argue that even if class-society happens to lead in the end to socialism, the price humanity has been forced to pay for this felicitous outcome is simply too high. How long would a socialist world have to survive, and how vigorously would it need to flourish, to justify in retrospect the sufferings of class-history? Could it ever do so, any more than one could justify Auschwitz? The Marxist philosopher Max Horkheimer comments that "history's route lies across the sorrow and misery of individuals. There is a series of explanatory connections between these two facts, but no justificatory meaning."[13]

Marxism is not generally seen as a tragic vision of the world. Its final Act—communism—appears too upbeat for that. But not to appreciate its tragic strain is to miss much of its complex depth. The Marxist narrative is not tragic in the sense of ending badly. But a narrative does not have to end badly to be tragic. Even if men and women find some fulfillment in the end, it is tragic that their ancestors had to be hauled through hell in order for them to do so. And there will be many who fall by the wayside, unfulfilled and unremembered. Short of some literal resurrection, we can never make recompense to these vanquished millions. Marx's theory of history is tragic in just this respect.

It is a quality well captured by Aijaz Ahmad. He is speaking of Marx on the destruction of the peasantry, but the point has a more general application to his work. There is, he writes, "a sense of colossal disruption and irretrievable loss, a moral dilemma wherein neither the old nor the new can be wholly affirmed, the recognition that the sufferer was at once decent and flawed, the recognition also that the history of victories and losses is really a history of material productions, and the glimmer of a hope, in the end, that something good might yet come of this merciless history."[14] Tragedy is not necessarily without hope. It is rather that when it affirms, it does so in fear and trembling, with a horror-stricken countenance.

There is, finally, another point to note. We have seen that Marx himself assumes that capitalism is indispensable for socialism. But is this true? What if one were to seek to develop the productive forces from a very low level, but as far as possible in ways compatible with democratic socialist values? It would be a fiercesomely difficult task. But this, roughly speaking, was the view of some members of the Left Opposition in Bolshevik Russia; and although it was a project that foundered, there is a strong case that it was the right strategy to adopt in the circumstances. What, in any case, if capitalism had never happened? Could not humanity have found some less atrocious way of evolving what Marx sees as its most precious goods—material prosperity, a wealth of creative human powers, self-determination, global communications, individual freedom, a magnificent culture and so on? Might an alternative history not have thrown up geniuses equal to Raphael and Shakespeare? One thinks of the flourishing of the arts and sciences in ancient Greece, Persia, Egypt, China, India, Mesopotamia and elsewhere. Was capitalist modernity really necessary? How does one weigh the value of modern science and human liberty against the spiritual goods of tribal societies? What happens when we place democracy in the scales along with the Holocaust?

The question may prove more than academic. Suppose a handful of us were to crawl out of the other side of a nuclear or environmental cataclysm, and begin the daunting task of building civilisation again from scratch. Given what we knew of the causes of the catastrophe, would we not be well-advised to try it this time the socialist way?

FOUR

Marxism is a dream of utopia. It believes in the possibility of a perfect society, without hardship, suffering, violence or conflict. Under communism there will be no rivalry, selfishness, possessiveness, competition or inequality. Nobody will be superior or inferior to anyone else. Nobody will work, human beings will live in complete harmony with one another, and the flow of material goods will be endless. This astonishingly naïve vision springs from a credulous faith in human nature. Human viciousness is simply set aside. The fact that we are naturally selfish, acquisitive, aggressive and competitive creatures, and that no amount of social engineering can alter this fact, is simply overlooked. Marx's dewy-eyed vision of the future reflects the absurd unreality of his politics as a whole.

"So will there still be road accidents in this Marxist utopia of yours?" This is the kind of sardonic inquiry that Marxists have grown used to dealing with. In fact, the comment reveals more about the ignorance of the speaker than about the illusions of the Marxist. Because if utopia means a perfect society, then "Marxist utopia" is a contradiction in terms.

There are, as it happens, far more interesting uses of the word "utopia" in the Marxist tradition.[1] One of the greatest of

English Marxist revolutionaries, William Morris, produced an unforgettable work of utopia in *News from Nowhere,* which unlike almost every other utopian work actually showed in detail how the process of political change had come about. When it comes to the everyday use of the word, however, it should be said that Marx shows not the slightest interest in a future free of suffering, death, loss, failure, breakdown, conflict, tragedy or even labour. In fact, he doesn't show much interest in the future at all. It is a notorious fact about his work that he has very little to say in detail about what a socialist or communist society would look like. His critics may therefore accuse him of unpardonable vagueness; but they can hardly do that and at the same time accuse him of drawing up utopian blueprints. It is capitalism, not Marxism, that trades in futures. In *The German Ideology,* he rejects the idea of communism as "an ideal to which reality will have to adjust itself." Instead, he sees it in *The German Ideology* as "the real movement which abolishes the present state of things."[2]

Just as the Jews were traditionally forbidden to foretell the future, so Marx the secular Jew is mostly silent on what might lie ahead. We have seen that he probably thought socialism was inevitable, but he has strikingly little to say about what it would look like. There are several reasons for this reticence. For one thing, the future does not exist, so that to forge images of it is a kind of lie. To do so might also suggest that the future is predetermined—that it lies in some shadowy realm for us to discover. We have seen that there is a sense in which Marx held that the future was inevitable. But the inevitable is not necessarily the desirable. Death is inevitable, too, but not in most people's eyes desirable. The future may be predetermined, but that is no reason to assume that it is going to be an improvement on what we have at the moment. The inevitable, as we have seen, is usually pretty unpleasant. Marx himself needed to be more aware of this.

Foretelling the future, however, is not only pointless; it can actually be destructive. To have power even over the future is a way of giving ourselves a false sense of security. It is a tactic for shielding ourselves from the open-ended nature of the present, with all its precariousness and unpredictability. It is to use the future as a kind of fetish—as a comforting idol to cling to like a toddler to its blanket. It is an absolute value which will not let us down because (since it does not exist) it is as insulated from the winds of history as a phantom. You can also seek to monopolise the future as a way of dominating the present. The true soothsayers of our time are not hairy, howling outcasts luridly foretelling the death of capitalism, but the experts hired by the transnational corporations to peer into the entrails of the system and assure its rulers that their profits are safe for another ten years. The prophet, by contrast, is not a clairvoyant at all. It is a mistake to believe that the biblical prophets sought to predict the future. Rather, the prophet denounces the greed, corruption and power-mongering of the present, warning us that unless we change our ways we might well have no future at all. Marx was a prophet, not a fortune-teller.

There is another reason why Marx was wary of images of the future. This is because there were a lot of them about in his time—and they were almost all the work of hopelessly idealist radicals. The idea that history is moving onwards and upwards to a state of perfection is not a leftist one. It was a commonplace of the eighteenth-century Enlightenment, which was hardly renowned for its revolutionary socialism. It reflected the confidence of the European middle class in its early, exuberant phase. Reason was in the process of vanquishing despotism, science was routing superstition, and peace was putting warfare to flight. As a result, the whole of human history (by which most of these thinkers really meant Europe) would culminate in a state of liberty, harmony and commercial prosperity. It is hardly likely that history's most celebrated scourge of the middle classes would have signed on for this self-satisfied illusion. Marx, as we have seen, did indeed believe in progress and civilisation; but he considered that, so far at least, they had proved inseparable from barbarism and benightedness.

This is not to say that Marx learnt nothing from utopian thinkers like Fourier, Saint-Simon and Robert Owen. If he could be rude about them, he could also commend their ideas, which were sometimes admirably progressive. (Not all of them, however. Fourier, who coined the term "feminism," and whose ideal social unit was designed to contain exactly 1,620 people, believed that in the future society the sea would turn into lemonade. Marx himself would probably have preferred a fine Riesling.) What Marx objected to among other things was the utopianists' belief that they could win over their opponents purely through the power of argument. Society for them was a battle of ideas, not a clash of material interests. Marx, by contrast, took a sceptical view of this faith in intellectual dialogue. He was aware that the ideas which really grip men and women arise through their routine practice, not through the discourse of philosophers or debating societies. If you want to see what men and women really believe, look at what they do, not at what they say.

Utopian blueprints for Marx were a distraction from the political tasks of the present. The energy invested in them could be used more fruitfully in the service of political struggle. As a materialist, Marx was chary of ideas which were divorced from historical reality, and thought that there were usually good historical reasons for this separation. Anyone with time on their hands can hatch elaborate schemes for a better future, just as anyone can sketch endless plans for a magnificent novel they never get around to writing because they are endlessly sketching plans for it. The point for Marx is not to dream of an ideal future, but to resolve the contradictions in the present which prevent a better future from coming about. When this has been achieved, there will be no more need for people like himself.

In *The Civil War in France,* Marx writes that the revolutionary workers "have no ideals to realize, but to set free the elements of the new society with which the old collapsing bourgeois society is itself pregnant."[3] The hope for a better future cannot just be a wistful "wouldn't it be nice if . . ." If it is to be more than an idle fantasy, a radically different future must be not only desirable but feasible; and to be feasible, it has to be anchored in the realities of the present. It cannot just be dropped into the present from some political outer space. There must be a way of scanning or X-raying the present which shows up a certain future as a potential within it. Otherwise, you will simply succeed in making people desire fruitlessly; and for Freud, to desire fruitlessly is to fall ill of neurosis.

So there are forces in the present which point beyond it. Feminism, for example, is a political movement at work right now; but it works by reaching for a future which would leave much of the present a long way behind. For Marx, it is the working class—at once a present reality and the agent by which it may be transformed—which provides the link between present and future. Emancipatory politics inserts the thin end of the wedge of the future into the heart of the present. They represent a bridge between present and future, a point where the two intersect. And both present and future are fuelled by the resources of the past, in the sense of precious political traditions which one must fight to keep alive.

Some conservatives are utopianists, but their utopia lies in the past rather than the future. In their view, history has been one long, doleful decline from a golden age set in the age of Adam, Virgil, Dante, Shakespeare, Samuel Johnson, Jefferson, Disraeli, Margaret Thatcher or more or less anyone you care to mention. This is to treat the past as a kind of fetish, rather as some utopian thinkers do with the future. The truth is that the past exists no more than the future, even though it feels as though it does. But there are also conservatives who reject this myth of the Fall on the grounds that every age has been just as dreadful as every other. The good news for them is that things are not getting worse; the bad news is that this is because they cannot deteriorate any further. What governs history is human nature, which is (a) in a state of shocking disrepair and (b) absolutely unalterable. The greatest folly—indeed, cruelty—is to dangle before men and women ideals that they are constitutionally incapable of achieving. Radicals just end up making people loathe themselves. They plunge them into guilt and despair in the act of cheering them on to higher things.

Starting from where we are may not sound the best recipe for political transformation. The present seems more an obstacle to such change than an occasion for it. As the stereotypically thick-headed Irishman remarked when asked the way to the railway station: "Well, I wouldn't start from here." The comment is not as illogical as some might think, which is also true of the Irish. It means "You'd get there quicker and more directly if you weren't starting from this awkward, out-of-the-way spot." Socialists today might well sympathise with the sentiment. One could imagine the proverbial Irishman surveying Russia after the Bolshevik revolution, about to embark on the task of building socialism in a besieged, isolated, semidestitute country, and remarking: "Well, I wouldn't start from here."

But there is, of course, nowhere else to start from. A different future has to be the future of this particular present. And most of the present is made up of the past. We have nothing with which to fashion a future other than the few, inadequate tools we have inherited from history. And these tools are tainted by the legacy of wretchedness and exploitation by which they descend to us. Marx writes in the *Critique of the Gotha Programme* of how the new society will be stamped with the birthmarks of the old order from whose womb it emerges. So there is no "pure" point from which to begin. To believe that there is is the illusion of so-called ultraleftism (an "infantile disorder," as Lenin called it), which in its revolutionary zeal refuses all truck with the compromised tools of the present: social reform, trade unions, political parties, parliamentary democracy and so on. It thus manages to end up as stainless as it is impotent.

The future, then, is not just to be tacked on to the present, any more than adolescence is just tacked on to childhood. It must somehow be detectable within it. This is not to say that this possible future is bound to come about, any more than a child will necessarily arrive at adolescence. It might always die of leukaemia before it does. It is rather to recognize that, given a particular present, not any old future is possible. The future is open, but it is not totally open. Not just any old thing could happen. Where I might be in ten minutes' time depends among other things on where I am now. To see the future as a potential within the present is not like seeing an egg as a potential chicken. Short of being smashed to smithereens or boiled for a picnic, the egg will turn into a chicken by a law of Nature; but Nature does not guarantee that socialism will follow on the heels of capitalism. There are many different futures implicit in the present, some of them a lot less attractive than others.

Seeing the future like this is among other things a safeguard against false images of it. It rejects, for example, the complacent "evolutionist" view of the future which regards it simply as more of the present. It is simply the present writ large. This, by and large, is the way our rulers like to view the future—as better than the present, but comfortably continuous with it. Disagreeable surprises will be kept to the minimum. There will be no traumas or cataclysms, just a steady improvement on what we have already. This view was known until recently as the End of History, before radical Islamists inconveniently broke History open again. You might also call it the goldfish theory of history, given that it dreams of an existence which is secure but monotonous, as the life of a goldfish appears to be. It pays for its freedom from dramatic shake-ups in the coinage of utter tedium. It thus fails to see that though the future may turn out to be a great deal worse than the present, the one sure thing about it is that it will be very different. One reason why the financial markets blew up a few years ago was because they relied on models that assumed the future would be very like the present.

Socialism, by contrast, represents in one sense a decisive break with the present. History has to be broken and remade —not because socialists arbitrarily prefer revolution to reform, being bloodthirsty beasts deaf to the voice of moderation, but because of the depth of the sickness that has to be cured. I say "history," but in fact Marx is reluctant to dignify everything that has happened so far with that title. For him, all we have known so far is "prehistory"—which is to say, one variation after another on human oppression and exploitation. The only truly historic act would be to break from this dreary narrative into history proper. As a socialist, you have to be prepared to spell out in some detail how this would be achieved, and what institutions it would involve. But if the new social order is to be genuinely transformative, it follows that there is a strict limit on how much you can say about it right now. We can, after all, describe the future only in terms drawn from the past or present; and a future which broke radically with the present would have us straining at the limits of our language. As Marx himself comments in *The Eighteenth Brumaire of Louis Bonaparte,* "There [in the socialist future] the content goes beyond the form." Raymond Williams makes essentially the same point in *Culture and Society 1780–1950,* when he writes: "We have to plan what can be planned, according to our common decision. But the emphasis of the idea of culture is right when it reminds us that a culture, essentially, is unplannable. We have to ensure the means of life, and the means of community. But what will then, by these means, be lived, we cannot know or say."[4]

One can put the point in another way. If all that has happened so far is "prehistory," then it is rather more predictable than what Marx would regard as history proper. If we slice through past history at any point and inspect a cross-section of it, we know before we have even come to look something of what we will find there. We will find, for example, that the great majority of men and women at this period are living lives of largely fruitless toil for the benefit of a ruling elite. We will find that the political state, whatever form it takes, is prepared to use violence from time to time to maintain this situation. We will find that quite a lot of the myth, culture and thought of the period provides some kind of legitimation of this situation. We will also probably find some form of resistance to this injustice among those who are exploited.

Once these shackles on human flourishing have been removed, however, it is far harder to say what will happen. For men and women are then a lot more free to behave as they wish, within the confines of their responsibility for one another. If they are able to spend more of their time in what we now call leisure activities rather than hard at work, their behavior becomes even harder to predict. I say "what we now call leisure" because if we really did use the resources accumulated by capitalism to release large numbers of people from work, we would not call what they did instead "leisure." This is because the idea of leisure depends on the existence of its opposite (labour), rather as you could not define warfare without some conception of peace. We should also remember that so-called leisure activities can be even more strenuous and exacting than coal mining. Marx himself makes this point. Some leftists will be disappointed to hear that not having to work does not necessarily mean lounging around the place all day smoking dope.

Take, as an analogy, the behavior of people in prison. It is fairly easy to say what prisoners get up to throughout the day because their activities are strictly regulated. The warders can predict with some certainty where they will be at five o'clock on a Wednesday, and if they cannot do so they might find themselves up before the Governor. Once convicts are released back into society, however, it is much harder to keep tabs on them, unless the tabs are of an electronic kind. They have moved, so to speak, from the "prehistory" of their incarceration to history proper, meaning that they are now at liberty to determine their own existence, rather than to have it determined for them by external forces. For Marx, socialism is the point where we begin collectively to determine our own destinies. It is democracy taken with full seriousness, rather than democracy as (for the most part) a political charade. And the fact that people are more free means that it will be harder to say what they will be doing at five o'clock on Wednesday.

A genuinely different future would be neither a mere extension of the present nor an absolute break with it. If it were an absolute break, how could we recognize it at all? Yet if we could describe it fairly easily in the language of the present, in what sense would it be genuinely different? Marx's idea of emancipation rejects both smooth continuities and total ruptures. In this sense, he is that rarest of creatures, a visionary who is also a sober realist. He turns from fantasies of the future to the prosaic workings of the present; but it is precisely there that he finds a greatly enriched future to be unleashed. He is more gloomy about the past than many thinkers, yet more hopeful than most of them about what is to come.

TERRY EAGLETON

Realism and vision here go hand in hand: to see the present as it truly is, is to see it in the light of its possible transformation. Otherwise you are simply not seeing it aright, as you would not have a full grasp of what it means to be a baby if you had not realized that it was a potential adult. Capitalism has given birth to extraordinary powers and possibilities which it simultaneously stymies; and this is why Marx can be hopeful without being a bright-eyed champion of Progress, and brutally realistic without being cynical or defeatist. It belongs to the tragic vision to stare the worst steadily in the face, but to rise above it through the very act of doing so. Marx, as we have seen, is in some ways a tragic thinker, which is not to say a pessimistic one.

On the one hand, Marxists are hardheaded types who are sceptical of high-minded moralism and wary of idealism. With their naturally suspicious minds, they tend to look for the material interests which lurk behind heady political rhetoric. They are alert to the humdrum, often ignoble forces which underlie pious talk and sentimental visions. Yet this is because they want to free men and women from these forces, in the belief that they are capable of better things. As such, they combine their hardheadedness with a faith in humanity. Materialism is too down-to-earth to be gulled by hand-on-heart rhetoric, but too hopeful that things could improve to be cynical. There have been worse combinations in the history of humanity.

Why Marx Was Right

One thinks of the flamboyant student slogan of Paris 1968: "Be realistic: demand the impossible!" For all its hyperbole, the slogan is accurate enough. What is realistically needed to repair society is beyond the powers of the prevailing system, and in that sense is impossible. But it is realistic to believe that the world could in principle be greatly improved. Those who scoff at the idea that major social change is possible are full-blown fantasists. The true dreamers are those who deny that anything more than piecemeal change can ever come about. This hardheaded pragmatism is as much a delusion as believing that you are Marie Antoinette. Such types are always in danger of being caught on the hop by history. Some feudal ideologues, for example, denied that an "unnatural" economic system like capitalism could ever catch on. There are also those sad, self-deceived characters who hallucinate that, given more time and greater effort, capitalism will deliver a world of abundance for all. For them, it is simply a regrettable accident that it has not done so so far. They do not see that inequality is as natural to capitalism as narcissism and megalomania are to Hollywood.

What Marx finds in the present is a deadly clash of interests. But whereas a utopian thinker might exhort us to rise above these conflicts in the name of love and fellowship, Marx himself takes a very different line. He does indeed believe in love and fellowship, but he does not think they will be achieved by some phoney harmony. The exploited and dispossessed are not to abandon their interests, which is just what their masters want them to do, but to press them all the way through. Only then might a society beyond self-interest finally emerge. There is nothing in the least wrong with being self-interested, if the alternative is hugging your chains in some false spirit of self-sacrifice.

Critics of Marx might find this stress on class interests distasteful. But they cannot claim in the same breath that he has an impossibly rosy view of human nature. Only by starting from the unredeemed present, submitting yourself to its degraded logic, can you hope to move through and beyond it. This, too, is in the traditional spirit of tragedy. Only by accepting that contradictions are of the nature of class-society, not by denying them in a spirit of serene disinterestedness, can you unlock the human wealth they hold back. It is at the points where the logic of the present comes unstuck, runs into impasse and incoherence, that Marx, surprisingly enough, finds the outline of a transfigured future. The true image of the future is the failure of the present.

Marxism, so many of its critics complain, has an impossibly idealized view of human nature. It dreams foolishly of a future in which everyone will be comradely and cooperative. Rivalry, envy, inequality, violence, aggression and competition will have been banished from the face of the earth. There is, in fact, scarcely a word in Marx's writings to support this outlandish claim, but a good few of his critics are reluctant to louse up their arguments with the facts. They are confident that Marx anticipated a state of human virtue known as communism which even the Archangel Gabriel might have a problem living up to. In doing so, he willfully or carelessly ignored that flawed, crooked, perpetually discontented state of affairs known as human nature.

Some Marxists have responded to this charge by claiming that if Marx overlooked human nature, it was because he did not believe in the idea. On this view, the concept of human nature is simply a way of keeping us politically in our place. It suggests that human beings are feeble, corrupt, self-interested creatures; that this remains unaltered throughout history; and that it is the rock on which any attempt at radical change will come to grief. "You can't change human nature" is one of the most common objections to revolutionary politics. Against this, some Marxists have insisted that there is no unchanging core to human beings. In their opinion, it is our history, not our nature, that makes us what we are; and since history is all about change, we can transform ourselves by altering our historical conditions.

Marx did not entirely subscribe to this "historicist" case. The evidence is that he did believe in a human nature, and was quite right to do so, as Norman Geras argues in an excellent little book.[5] He did not see this as overriding the importance of the individual. On the contrary, he thought it a paradoxical feature of our common nature that we are all uniquely individuated. In his early writings, Marx speaks of what he calls human "species being," which is really a materialist version of human nature. Because of the nature of our material bodies, we are needy, labouring, sociable, sexual, communicative, self-expressive animals who need one another to survive, but who come to find a fulfillment in that companionship over and above its social usefulness. If I may be allowed to quote a previous comment of my own: "If another creature is able in principle to speak to us, engage in material labour alongside us, sexually interact with us, produce something which looks vaguely like art in the sense that it appears fairly pointless, suffer, joke and die, then we can deduce from these biological facts a huge number of moral and even political consequences."[6] This case, which is technically known as a philosophical anthropology, is rather out of fashion these days; but it was what Marx argued for in his early work, and there is no compelling reason to believe that he abandoned it later on.

Because we are labouring, desiring, linguistic creatures, we are able to transform our conditions in the process we know as history. In doing so, we come to transform ourselves at the same time. Change, in other words, is not the opposite of human nature; it is possible because of the creative, open-ended, unfinished beings we are. This, as far as we can tell, is not true of stoats. Because of the nature of their material bodies, stoats do not have a history. Nor do stoats have politics, unless they are keeping them cunningly concealed. There is no reason to fear that they might one day come to rule over us, even if they would probably do a far better job than our present leaders. As far as we know, they cannot be social democrats or ultranationalists. Human beings, however, are political animals by their very nature—not only because they live in community with one another, but because they need some system for regulating their material life. They also need some system for regulating their sexual lives. One reason for this is that sexuality might otherwise prove too socially disruptive. Desire, for example, is no respecter of social distinctions. But this is also one reason why human beings need politics. The way they produce their material existence has so far involved exploitation and inequality, and a political system is needed to contain the resulting conflicts. We would also expect human animals to have various symbolic ways of representing all this to themselves, whether we call it art, myth or ideology.

For Marx, we are equipped by our material natures with certain powers and capacities. And we are at our most human when we are free to realize these powers as an end in itself, rather than for any purely utilitarian purpose. These powers and capacities are always historically specific; but they have a foundation in our bodies, and some of them alter very little from one human culture to another. Two individuals from very different cultures who do not speak one another's language can easily cooperate in practical tasks. This is because the physical body they have in common generates its own set of assumptions, expectations and understandings.[7] All human cultures know grief and ecstasy, labour and sexuality, friendship and enmity, oppression and injustice, sickness and mortality, kinship and art. It is true that they sometimes know these things in very different cultural styles. Dying is not the same in Madras as it is in Manchester. But we die anyway. Marx himself writes in the *Economic and Philosophical Manuscripts* that "man as an objective, sensuous being is therefore a *suffering* being—and because he feels that he suffers, a *passionate* being." Death, he considers, is a harsh victory of the species over the individual. It matters to men and women, he writes in *Capital,* if their deaths are premature, their lives shorter than they need be because of grinding toil, or afflicted by accident, injury or disease. Communism may see an end to grinding toil, but it is hard to believe that Marx envisages a social order without accident, injury and disease, any more than he anticipates one without death.

If we did not share so much basic common humanity, the socialist vision of global cooperation would be fruitless. Marx speaks in volume 1 of *Capital* of "human nature in general and then . . . as modified in each historical epoch." There is a great deal about human beings that hardly varies across history—a fact which postmodernism either denies or dismisses as merely trivial. It does so partly because it has an irrational prejudice against Nature and biology; partly because it thinks that all talk of natures is a way of denying change;[8] and partly because it tends to regard all change as positive and all permanence as negative. In this last opinion, it is at one with capitalist "modernisers" everywhere. The truth—far too banal for intellectuals to appreciate—is that some change is catastrophic and some kinds of permanence deeply desirable. It would be a shame, for example, if all French vineyards were to be burnt down tomorrow, just as it would be a pity if a nonsexist society lasted for only three weeks.

Socialists often speak of oppression, injustice and exploitation. But if this were all humanity had ever known, we would never be able to identify these things for what they are. Instead, they would simply seem like our natural condition. We might not even have special names for them. To see a relationship as exploitative, you need to have some idea of what a nonexploitative relationship would look like. You do not need to appeal to the idea of human nature to have this. You can appeal to historical factors instead. But it is plausible to claim that there are features of our nature which act as a kind of norm in this respect. Human beings, for example, are all "prematurely" born. For a long time after birth they are unable to fend for themselves, and are thus in need of a prolonged period of nurturing. (It is this unusually prolonged experience of care, some psychoanalysts argue, that plays such havoc with our psyches later in life. If babies could get up and walk away at birth, a good deal of adult misery would be avoided, and not only in the sense that there would be no bawling brats to disturb our sleep.) Even if the care they receive is appalling, infants very quickly imbibe some notion of what caring for others means. This is one reason why, later on, they may be able to identify a whole way of life as callously indifferent to human needs. In this sense, we can move from being prematurely born to politics.

Needs which are essential to our survival and well-being, like being fed, keeping warm and sheltered, enjoying the company of others, not being enslaved or abused and so on, can act as a basis for political critique, in the sense that any society which fails to meet these requirements is clearly lacking. We can, of course, object to such societies on more local or cultural grounds. But arguing that they violate some of the most fundamental demands of our nature has even more force. So it is a mistake to think that the idea of human nature is just an apology for the status quo. It can also act as a powerful challenge to it.

In early writings like the *Economic and Philosophical Manuscripts of 1844*, Marx holds to the currently unfashionable view that the way we are as material animals can tell us something important about how we should live. There is a sense in which you can get from the human body to questions of ethics and politics. If human beings are self-realising creatures, then they need to be at liberty to fulfill their needs and express their powers. But if they are also social animals, living alongside other self-expressive beings, they need to prevent an endless, destructive clash of these powers. This, in fact, is one of the most intractable problems of liberal society, in which individuals are supposed to be free, but free among other things to be constantly at one another's throats. Communism, by contrast, organises social life so that individuals are able to realize themselves in and through the self-realisation of others. As Marx puts it in the *Communist Manifesto,* "The free development of each becomes the condition for the free development of all." In this sense, socialism does not simply reject liberal society, with its passionate commitment to the individual. Instead, it builds on and completes it. In doing so, it shows how some of the contradictions of liberalism, in which your freedom may flourish only at the expense of mine, may be resolved. Only through others can we finally come into our own. This means an enrichment of individual freedom, not a diminishing of it. It is hard to think of a finer ethics. On a personal level, it is known as love.

It is worth stressing Marx's concern with the individual, since it runs clean contrary to the usual caricature of his work. In this view, Marxism is all about faceless collectives which ride roughshod over personal life. Nothing, in fact, could be more alien to Marx's thought. One might say that the free flourishing of individuals is the whole aim of his politics, as long as we remember that these individuals must find some way of flourishing in common. To assert one's individuality, he writes in *The Holy Family,* is "the vital manifestation of [one's] being." This, one might claim, is Marx's morality from start to finish.

There is good reason to suspect that there can never be any complete reconciliation between individual and society. The dream of an organic unity between them is a generous-hearted fantasy. There will always be conflicts between my fulfillment and yours, or between what is required of me as a citizen and what I badly want to do. Such outright contradictions are the stuff of tragedy, and only the grave, as opposed to Marxism, can put us beyond that condition. Marx's claim in the *Communist Manifesto* about the free self-development of all can never be fully realised. Like all the finest ideals it is a goal to aim at, not a state to be literally achieved. Ideals are signposts, not tangible entities. They point us the way to go. Those who scoff at socialist ideals should remember that the free market can never be perfectly realized either. Yet this does not stop free-marketeers in their tracks. The fact that there is no flawless democracy does not lead most of us to settle for tyranny instead. We do not relinquish efforts to feed the hungry of the world because we know some of them will have perished before we can do so. Some of those who claim that socialism is unworkable are confident that they can eradicate poverty, solve the global warming crisis, spread liberal democracy to Afghanistan and resolve world conflicts by United Nations resolutions. All these daunting tasks are comfortably within the range of the possible. It is only socialism which for some mysterious reason is out of reach.

It is easier to attain Marx's goal, however, if you do not have to rely on everyone being morally magnificent all the time. Socialism is not a society which requires resplendent virtue of its citizens. It does not mean that we have to be wrapped around each other all the time in some great orgy of togetherness. This is because the mechanisms which would allow Marx's goal to be approached would actually be built into social institutions. They would not rely in the first place on the goodwill of the individual. Take, for example, the idea of a self-governing cooperative, which Marx seems to have regarded as the key productive unit of the socialist future. One person's contribution to such an outfit allows for some kind of self-realisation; but it also contributes to the well-being of the others, and this simply by virtue of the way the place is set up. I do not have to have tender thoughts about my fellow workers, or whip myself into an altruistic frenzy every two hours. My own self-realisation helps to enhance theirs simply because of the cooperative, profit-sharing, egalitarian, commonly governed nature of the unit. It is a structural affair, not a question of personal virtue. It does not demand a race of Cordelias.

TERRY EAGLETON

For some socialist purposes, then, it does not matter if I am the vilest worm in the West. In a similar way, it does not matter if I regard my work as a biochemist employed by a private pharmaceutical company as a glorious contribution to the advance of science and the progress of humanity. The fact remains that the main point of my work is to create profit for a bunch of unscrupulous sharks who would probably charge their own toddlers ten dollars for an aspirin. What I feel is neither here nor there. The meaning of my work is determined by the institution.

One would expect any socialist institution to have its fair share of chancers, toadies, bullies, cheats, loafers, scroungers, freeloaders, free riders and occasional psychopaths. Nothing in Marx's writing suggests that this would not be so. Besides, if communism is about everyone participating as fully as possible in social life, then one would expect there to be more conflicts rather than fewer, as more individuals get in on the act. Communism would not spell the end of human strife. Only the literal end of history would do that. Envy, aggression, domination, possessiveness and competition would still exist. It is just that they could not take the forms they assume under capitalism—not because of some superior human virtue, but because of a change of institutions.

These vices would no longer be bound up with the exploitation of child labour, colonial violence, grotesque social inequalities and cutthroat economic competition. Instead, they would have to assume some other form. Tribal societies have their fair share of violence, rivalry and hunger for power, but these things cannot take the form of imperial warfare, free-market competition or mass unemployment, because such institutions do not exist among the Nuer or the Dinka. There are villains everywhere you look, but only some of these moral ruffians are so placed as to be able to steal pension funds or pump the media full of lying political propaganda. Most gangsters are not in a position to do so. Instead, they have to content themselves with hanging people from meat hooks. In a socialist society, nobody would be in a position to do so. This is not because they would be too saintly, but because there would be no private pension funds or privately owned media. Shakespeare's villains had to find outlets for their wickedness other than firing missiles at Palestinian refugees. You cannot be a bullying industrial magnate if there isn't any industry around. You just have to settle for bullying slaves, courtiers or your Neolithic workmates instead.

Or consider the practice of democracy. It is true that there are always monstrous egoists who try to browbeat others, as well as people who seek to bribe or smooth-talk their way to power. Democracy, however, is a set of built-in safeguards against such behavior. By devices such as one-person-one-vote, chairpersons, amendments, accountability, due procedure, the sovereignty of the majority and so on, you do your best to ensure that the bullies cannot win. From time to time they will succeed in doing just that. They might even manage to suborn the whole process. But having an established process means that most of the time they will be forced to submit to the democratic consensus. Virtue, so to speak, is built into the proceedings, not left to the vagaries of individual character. You do not need to make people physically incapable of violence in order to end a war. You just need negotiations, disarmament, peace treaties, monitoring and the like. This can be difficult. But it is not half as difficult as breeding a race of people who would vomit and swoon at the slightest sign of aggression.

So Marxism holds out no promise of human perfection. It does not even promise to abolish hard labour. Marx seems to believe that a certain amount of disagreeable work would continue to be essential even in conditions of plenty. The curse of Adam will linger on even in the realm of abundance. The promise Marxism does hold out is to resolve the contradictions which currently stop history proper from happening, in all its freedom and diversity.

The aims of Marxism, however, are not just material. For Marx, communism means an end to scarcity, along with an end to most oppressive labour. But the freedom and leisure which this would grant men and women can then provide the context for their fuller spiritual flourishing. It is true, as we have seen, that spiritual and material development by no means always march side by side. One has only to look at Keith Richards to recognize that. There are many kinds of material affluence which spell the death of the spirit. Yet it is also true that you cannot be free to become what you want when you are starving, sorely oppressed or stunted in your moral growth by a life of endless drudgery. Materialists are not those who deny the spiritual, but those who remind us that spiritual fulfillment requires certain material conditions. Those conditions do not guarantee such fulfillment. But it cannot be had without them.

Human beings are not at their best in conditions of scarcity, whether natural or artificial. Such scarcity breeds violence, fear, greed, anxiety, possessiveness, domination and deadly antagonism. One would expect, then, that if men and women were able to live in conditions of material abundance, released from these crippling pressures, they would tend to fare better as moral beings than they do now. We cannot be sure of this because we have never known such conditions. This is what Marx has in mind when he declares in the *Communist Manifesto* that the whole of history has been the history of class struggle. And even in conditions of abundance there would be plenty of other things for us to feel anxious, aggressive and possessive about. We would not be alchemized into angels. But some of the root causes of our moral deficiencies would have been removed. To that extent, it is indeed reasonable to claim that a communist society would tend by and large to produce finer human beings than we can muster at the moment. But they would still be fallible, prone to conflict and sometimes brutal and malevolent.

Cynics who doubt that such moral progress is possible should consider the difference between burning witches and pressing for equal pay for women. That is not to say that we have all become more delicate, sensitive and humanitarian than we were in medieval times. As far as that goes, we might also consider the difference between bows and arrows and Cruise missiles. The point is not that history as a whole has morally improved. It is simply that we have made major progress here and there. It is as soberly realistic to recognize this fact as it is reasonable to claim that in some ways we have deteriorated since the days of Robin Hood. There is no grand narrative of Progress, just as there is no fairy tale of Decline.

Anyone who has witnessed a small infant snatch a toy from its sibling with a bloodcurdling cry of "Mine!" needs no reminder of how deep in the mind the roots of rivalry and possessiveness sink. We are speaking of ingrained cultural, psychological and even evolutionary habits, which no mere change of institutions will alter in itself. But social change does not depend on everyone revolutionising their attitudes overnight. Take the example of Northern Ireland. Peace did not come to this tumultuous region because Catholics and Protestants finally abandoned their centuries-old antagonism and fell fondly into each others' arms. Far from it. Some of them will continue to detest each other as far into the future as one can see. Changes in sectarian consciousness are likely to be geologically slow. Yet in one sense this is not all that important. What was important was securing a political agreement which could be carefully policed and skillfully evolved, in the context of a general public weariness with thirty years of violence.

That, however, is only one side of the story. For the truth is that over long periods of time, changes of institution do indeed have profound effects on human attitudes. Almost every enlightened penal reform history has achieved was bitterly resisted in its day; but we now take these changes so much for granted that we would be revolted by the idea of breaking murderers on a wheel. Such reforms have become built into our psyches. What really alters our view of the world is not so much ideas, as ideas which are embedded in routine social practice. If we change that practice, which may be formidably difficult to do, we are likely in the end to alter our way of seeing.

Most of us do not have to be forcibly restrained from relieving ourselves on crowded streets. Because there is a law against it, and because it is socially frowned on, not to do so has become second nature to us. This is not to say that none of us ever do it, not least in city centres when the pubs have just closed. It is just that we are a lot less likely to do it than if it were considered the height of elegance. The British injunction to drive on the left does not have to struggle in the breasts of Britishers with a burning desire to drive on the right. Institutions shape our inner experience. They are instruments of reeducation. We shake hands on first meeting partly because it is the conventional thing to do, but also because, being the conventional thing to do, we feel an impulse to do it.

These changes of habit take a long time. It took some centuries for capitalism to root out modes of feeling inherited from feudalism, and a tourist outside Buckingham Palace might well consider that some vital areas were carelessly overlooked. It would not, one hopes, take quite so long to produce a social order in which schoolchildren studying history would greet with utter incredulity the fact that once upon a time millions of people went hungry while a handful of others fed caviar to their poodles. It would seem as alien and repellent to them as the thought of disembowelling a man for heresy now seems to us.

To mention schoolchildren raises an important point. A great many children today are fervent environmentalists. They regard the clubbing to death of seals or the pollution of the atmosphere with horror and disgust. Some of them would even be appalled by the dropping of a piece of litter. And this is largely because of education—not just formal education, but the influence of new forms of thought and feeling on a generation in which old habits of feeling are less entrenched. No one is arguing that this will save the planet. And it is true that there are children who would cheerfully brain a badger. Even so, there is evidence here of how education can change attitudes and breed new forms of behavior.

Political education, then, is always possible. At a conference in Britain in the early 1970s, a discussion took place over whether there were certain universal features of human beings. One man stood up and announced "Well, we've all got testicles." A woman in the audience shouted out "No, we haven't!" Feminism in Britain was still in its early days, and the remark was greeted by a good many men in the room as merely eccentric. Even some of the women looked embarrassed. Only a few years later, if a man had made such a fatuous statement in public, he might rapidly have become the only exception to his claim.

In medieval and early-modern Europe, avarice was regarded as the foulest of vices. From that to the Wall Street slogan "greed is good!" involved an intensive process of re-education. What did the reeducating was not in the first place schoolteachers or propagandists but changes in our material forms of life. Aristotle thought slavery was natural, though some other ancient thinkers did not agree. But he also thought it contrary to human nature to gear economic production to profit, which is not quite the opinion of Donald Trump. (Aristotle held this view for an interesting reason. He thought that what Marx was later to call "exchange-value"—the way that one commodity can be exchanged with another, and that with another, and so on ad infinitum—involves a kind of bound-lessness which was foreign to the finite, creaturely nature of human beings.) There were medieval ideologues who viewed profit-making as unnatural, because human nature for them meant feudal nature. Hunter-gatherers probably took an equally dim view of the possibility of any social order but their own. Alan Greenspan, former chairman of the U.S. Federal Reserve, believed for much of his professional life that so-called free markets were rooted in human nature, a claim as absurd as holding that admiring Cliff Richard is rooted in human nature. Free markets are in fact a recent historical invention, and were confined for a long time to a minor region of the globe.

Similarly, those who speak of socialism as contrary to human nature do so because in their myopic way they iden-tify that nature with capitalism. The Tuareg people of the central Sahara are really capitalist entrepreneurs at heart. They would secretly like nothing better than to start up an investment bank. The fact that they do not even have the concept of an investment bank is neither here nor there. But one cannot desire something of which one has no notion. I cannot hanker to become a stockbroker if I am an Athenian slave. I can be rapacious, acquisitive and religiously devoted to my own self-interest. But I cannot be a closet capitalist, just as I cannot aspire to be a brain surgeon if I am living in the eleventh century.

Why Marx Was Right

I claimed before that Marx, rather strangely, was both unusually pessimistic about the past and unusually optimistic about the future. There are several reasons for this, but one of them in particular bears on the issues we are examining. Marx was gloomy about much of the past because it seemed to represent one wretched form of oppression and exploitation after another. Theodor Adorno once remarked that pessimistic thinkers (he had Freud rather than Marx in mind) do more service to the cause of human emancipation than callowly optimistic ones. This is because they bear witness to an injustice which cries out for redemption, and which we might otherwise forget. By reminding us of how bad things are, they prompt us to repair them. They urge us to do without opium.

If Marx also retained a good deal of hope for the future, however, it was because he recognized that this dismal record was not for the most part our fault. If history has been so bloody, it is not because most human beings are wicked. It is because of the material pressures to which they have been submitted. Marx can thus take a realistic measure of the past without succumbing to the myth of the darkness of men's hearts. And this is one reason why he can retain faith in the future. It is his materialism which permits him that hope. If wars, famines and genocide really did spring simply from some unchanging human depravity, then there is not the slightest reason to believe that the future will fare any better. If, however, these things have been partly the effect of unjust social systems, of which individuals are sometimes little more than functions, then it is reasonable to expect that changing that system may make for a better world. The bugbear of perfection, meanwhile, can be left to frighten fools.

This is not to suggest that men and women in class-society can be absolved of all blame for their actions, or that individual depravity has played no part in wars and genocides. Companies which consign hundreds or even thousands of workers to a life of enforced idleness can most certainly be blamed. But it is not as though they take such measures out of hatred, malice or aggression. They create unemployment because they want to safeguard their profits in a competitive system in which they fear they might otherwise go under. Those who order armies to war, where they may end up burning small children to death, may be the meekest of men. Even so, Nazism was not just a noxious political system; it also drew on the sadism, paranoia and pathological hatred of individuals who could genuinely be described as wicked. If Hitler was not wicked, then the term has no meaning. But their personal viciousness could only have the appalling results it did because it was yoked to the workings of a political system. It would be like putting Shakespeare's Iago in charge of a prisoner-of-war camp.

If there is indeed a human nature, then this is in some ways good news, whatever the postmodernists might think. This is because one fairly consistent feature of that nature has been a resistance to injustice. This is one reason why it is foolish to imagine that the idea of human nature must always work in conservative ways. Surveying the historical record, it is not hard to conclude that political oppression has almost always incited rebellion, however subdued or unsuccessful. There seems to be something in humanity which will not bow meekly to the insolence of power. It is true that power only really succeeds by winning the collusion of its underlings. The evidence, however, is that this collusion is usually partial, ambiguous and provisional. Ruling classes are generally more tolerated than admired. If our nature is purely cultural, then there is no reason why political regimes should not mould us into accepting their authority without question. That they often find this extraordinarily difficult to do testifies to sources of resistance which run deeper than local cultures.

So was Marx a utopian thinker? Yes, if by that one means that he envisaged a future which would be a vast improvement on the present. He believed in the end of material scarcity, private property, exploitation, social classes and the state as we know it. Yet many thinkers, casting an eye over the accumulated resources of the world today, would judge abolishing material scarcity to be perfectly reasonable in principle, however hard it is to achieve in practice. It is politics that stands in our way.

As we have seen, Marx also considered that this would

involve the emancipation of human, spiritual wealth on a major scale. Freed from former constraints, men and women would flourish as individuals in ways impossible to them before. But there is nothing in Marx's work to suggest that we would thereby arrive at any sort of perfection. It is a condition of exercising their freedom that human beings are able to abuse it. In fact, there cannot be such freedom, on any sizeable scale, without such abuses. So it is reasonable to believe that in communist society there would be plenty of problems, a host of conflicts and a number of irreparable tragedies. There would be child murders, road accidents, wretchedly bad novels, lethal jealousies, overweening ambitions, tasteless trousers and inconsolable grief. There might also be some cleaning of the latrines.

Communism is about the fulfillment of everyone's needs, but even in a society of abundance, this would need to be restricted. As Norman Geras points out, "If by way of means of self-development (under communism) you need a violin and I need a racing bicycle, this, one may assume, will be all right. But if I need an enormously large area, say Australia, to wander around in or generally use it as I see fit undisturbed by the presence of other people, then this obviously will not be all right. No conceivable abundance could satisfy needs of self-development of this magnitude . . . and it is not difficult to think of needs much less excessive of which the same will be true."[9]

Why Marx Was Right

Marx, as we have seen, treats the future not as a matter of idle speculation, but as a feasible extrapolation from the present. He is concerned not with poetic visions of peace and comradeship, but with the material conditions which might allow a truly human future to emerge. As a materialist, he was alert to the complex, recalcitrant, unfinished nature of reality; and such a world is incompatible with a vision of perfection. A perfect world would be one which had abolished all contingency—all of those random collisions, chance occurrences and tragically unforeseeable effects which make up the texture of our daily lives. It would also be one in which we could do justice to the dead as well as the living, undoing the crimes and repairing the horrors of the past. No such society is possible. Nor would it necessarily be desirable. A world without train crashes might also be one without the possibility of a cure for cancer.

Neither is it possible to have a social order in which everyone is equal. The complaint that "socialism would make us all the same" is baseless. Marx had no such intention. He was a sworn enemy of uniformity. In fact, he regarded equality as a *bourgeois* value. He saw it as a reflection in the political sphere of what he called exchange-value, in which one commodity is levelled in value with another. The commodity, he once commented, is "realised equality." He speaks at one point of a kind of communism that involves a general social leveling, and denounces it in the *Economic and Philosophical*

Manuscripts as "an abstract negation of the entire world of culture and civilisation." Marx also associated the notion of equality with what he saw as the abstract equality of middle-class democracy, where our formal equality as voters and citizens serves to obscure real inequalities of wealth and class. In the *Critique of the Gotha Programme,* he also rejected the idea of an equality of income, since people have uniquely different needs: some do more dirty or dangerous work than others, some have more children to feed, and so on.

This is not to say that he dismissed the idea of equality out of hand. Marx was not in the habit of writing off ideas simply because they were of middle-class provenance. Far from contemptuously spurning the ideals of middle-class society, he was a doughty champion of its great revolutionary values of freedom, self-determination and self-development. Even abstract equality, he considered, was a welcome advance on the hierarchies of feudalism. It was just that he thought that these precious values had no chance of working for everyone as long as capitalism still existed. Even so, he lavished praise upon the middle class as the most revolutionary formation that history had ever witnessed, a fact that his middle-class opponents tend curiously to overlook. Perhaps they suspect that to be praised by Marx is the ultimate kiss of death.

In Marx's view, what was awry with the prevailing notion of equality was that it was too abstract. It did not pay sufficient attention to the individuality of things and people—

what Marx called in the economic realm "use-value." It was capitalism that standardised people, not socialism. This is one reason why Marx was rather chary of the notion of rights. "Right," he comments, "by its very nature can consist only in the application of an equal standard; but unequal individuals (and they would not be different individuals if they were not unequal) are measurable by an equal standard only in so far as they are brought under an equal point of view, are taken from one *definite* side only, for instance, in the present case, regarded only as *workers* and nothing more is seen in them, everything else is ignored."[10] So much, then, for the Marx who wants to reduce us all to the same dead level. So much also for the Marx who when he looks at people can see nothing but workers. Equality for socialism does not mean that everyone is just the same—an absurd proposition if ever there was one. Even Marx would have noticed that he was more intelligent than the Duke of Wellington. Nor does it mean that everyone will be granted exactly the same amount of wealth or resources.

Genuine equality means not treating everyone the same, but attending equally to everyone's different needs. And this is the kind of society which Marx looked forward to. Human needs are not all commensurate with one another. You cannot measure them all by the same yardstick. Everyone for Marx was to have an equal right to self-realisation, and to participate actively in the shaping of social life. Barriers of inequality would thus be broken down. But the result of this would be as far as possible to allow each person to flourish as the unique individual they were. In the end, equality for Marx exists for the sake of difference. Socialism is not about everyone wearing the same kind of boiler suit. It is consumer capitalism which decks out its citizens in uniforms known as tracksuits and trainers.

In Marx's view, socialism would thus constitute a far more pluralistic order than the one we have now. In class-society, the free self-development of the few is bought at the cost of the shackling of the many, who then come to share much the same monotonous narrative. Communism, precisely because everyone would be encouraged to develop their individual talents, would be a great deal more diffuse, diverse and unpredictable. It would be more like a modernist novel than a realist one. Critics of Marx may scorn this as a fantasy. But they cannot complain at the same time that Marx's preferred social order looks much like the one in George Orwell's *Nineteen Eighty-Four*.

A virulent form of utopianism has indeed afflicted the modern age, but its name is not Marxism. It is the crazed notion that a single global system known as the free market can impose itself on the most diverse cultures and economies and cure all their ills. The purveyors of this totalitarian fantasy are not to be found hiding scar-faced and sinisterly soft-spoken in underground bunkers like James Bond villains.

They are to be seen dining at upmarket Washington restaurants and strolling on Sussex estates.

Theodor Adorno's answer to the question of whether Marx was a utopian thinker is a decisive yes and no. He was, Adorno writes, an enemy of utopia for the sake of its realization.

FIVE

Marxism reduces everything to economics. It is a form of economic determinism. Art, religion, politics, law, war, morality, historical change: all these are seen in the crudest terms as nothing more than reflections of the economy or class struggle. The true complexity of human affairs is passed over for a monochrome vision of history. In his obsession with economics, Marx was simply an inverted image of the capitalist system he opposed. His thought is at odds with the pluralist outlook of modern societies, conscious as they are that the varied range of historical experience cannot be crammed into a single rigid framework.

In one sense, the claim that everything comes down to economics is surely a truism. In fact, it is so blindingly obvious that it is hard to see how anyone could doubt it. Before we can do anything else, we need to eat and drink. We also need clothing and shelter, at least if we are living in Sheffield rather than Samoa. The first historical act, Marx writes in *The German Ideology,* is the production of the means to satisfy our material needs. Only then can we learn to play the banjo, write erotic poetry or paint the front porch. The basis of culture is labour. There can be no civilisation without material production.

Marxism, however, wants to claim more than this. It wants to argue that material production is fundamental not only in the sense that there could be no civilisation without it, but that it is what ultimately determines the nature of that civilisation. There is a difference between saying that a pen or computer is indispensable to writing a novel, and claiming that it somehow determines the content of the novel. The latter case is by no means blindingly obvious, even though the Marxist equivalent of it has the support of some anti-Marxist thinkers as well. The philosopher John Gray, who is scarcely an apologist for Marxism, writes that "in market societies ... not only is economic activity distinct from the rest of social life, but it conditions, and sometimes dominates, the whole of society."[1] What Gray confines to market societies, Marx generalizes to human history as such.

Critics of Marx regard the stronger of the two claims as a form of reductionism. It boils everything down to the same factor. And this seems clearly wrongheaded. How could the stunning variety of human history be straitjacketed in this way? Surely there is a plurality of forces at work in history, which can never be reduced to a single, unchanging principle? We might wonder, however, how far this kind of pluralism is prepared to go. Is there *never* any single factor in historical situations which is more important than the others? This is surely hard to swallow. We might argue till Doomsday about the causes of the French Revolution, but nobody thinks that it broke out because of biochemical changes in the French brain brought about by too much cheese-eating. Only a seriously weird minority claims that it happened because Aries was in the ascendant. Everyone agrees that some historical factors are more weighty than others. This does not prevent them from being pluralists, at least in one sense of the word. They might still accept that every major historical event is the upshot of a multiplicity of forces. It is just that they are reluctant to assign all these forces the same importance.

Friedrich Engels was a pluralist in just this sense. He vehemently denied that he and Marx ever meant to suggest that economic forces were the sole determinant of history. That, he considered, was a "meaningless, abstract, senseless phrase."[2] The truth is that nobody is a pluralist in the sense of holding that in any given situation, any factor is as vital as any other. Everyone believes in hierarchies, even the most fervent of egalitarians. In fact, almost everyone believes in absolute, unchanging hierarchies. It is hard to find anyone who thinks that tickling the starving is ever preferable to feeding them. Nobody contends that the length of Charles I's fingernails was a more decisive factor than religion in the English Civil War. There were lots of reasons for my holding your head underwater for twenty minutes (sadism, scientific curiosity, that appalling flowery shirt you were wearing, the fact that there was only a boring old documentary on television), but the overriding reason was to get my hands on the stable of prize-winning horses you had bequeathed me in your will. Why should public events not have overriding motives too?

Some pluralists agree that such events may result from a single predominant cause. It is just that they do not see why the same cause should be operative in every case. Surely what is implausible about the so-called economic theory of history is the idea that everything, everywhere, is conditioned in just the same way. Doesn't this suggest that history is a single phenomenon, as miraculously uniform all the way through as a stick of rock? It makes sense to suppose that the cause of my headache was that ridiculously tight Marilyn Monroe wig I insisted on wearing to the party; but history is not a single thing like a headache. As the man complained, it is just one damn thing after another. It does not have the consistency of a fairy tale, or form a coherent narrative. There is no unbroken thread of meaning running all the way through it.

We have seen already that scarcely anybody imagines that there are no intelligible patterns in history at all. It is rare to find someone who sees history as simply one shambolic heap of chaos, chance, accident and contingency, though Friedrich Nietzsche and his disciple Michel Foucault sail close to this view at times. Most people accept that there are chains of cause and effect in history, however complex or hard to fathom, and that this lends it some rough kind of pattern. It is hard to believe, for example, that various nations began to collect colonies at a certain historical point for reasons that had nothing whatsoever in common. African slaves were not transported to America for no reason at all. That fascism emerged at more or less the same time in various twentieth-century nations was not just a copycat affair. People do not suddenly hurl themselves on open fires just for the hell of it. There is a remarkably uniform pattern across the globe of people pointedly not doing so.

The question, surely, is not whether there are patterns in history, but whether there is one predominant pattern. You can believe the former without crediting the latter. Why not just a set of overlapping designs that never merge into a whole? How on earth could something as diverse as human history form a unified story? To contend that material interests have been the prime mover all the way from the cave dwellers to capitalism is a lot more plausible than believing that diet, altruism, Great Men, pole-vaulting or the conjunction of the planets has been. But it still seems too singular an answer to be satisfying.

If it is satisfying to Marx, it is because he considers that history has been by no means as varied and colourful as it may appear. It has been a much more monotonous story than meets the eye. There is indeed a kind of unity to it; but it is not one that should yield us any pleasure, as the unity of *Bleak House* or *High Noon* might. For the most part, the threads that leash it together have been scarcity, hard labour, violence and exploitation. And though these things have taken very different forms, they have so far laid the foundation of every civilisation on record. It is this dull, mind-numbing recurrence that has lent human history a good deal more consistency than we might desire. There is indeed a grand narrative here, and more's the pity. As Theodor Adorno observes, "The One and All that keeps rolling on to this day—with occasional breathing spells—would teleologically be the absolute of suffering." The grand narrative of history is not one of Progress, Reason or Enlightenment. It is a melancholic tale which leads in Adorno's words "from the slingshot to the atomic bomb."[3]

It is possible to agree that violence, hard labour and exploitation bulk large in human history without accepting that they are the foundation of it. For Marxists, one reason why they are so fundamental is that they are bound up with our physical survival. They have been abiding features of the way we maintain our material existence. They are not just random events. We are not speaking of scattered acts of savagery or aggression. If there has been a certain necessity to these things, it is because they are built into the structures by which we produce and reproduce our material life. Even so, no Marxist imagines that these forces shape absolutely everything. If they did, then typhoid, ponytails, convulsive laughter, Sufism, the *Saint Matthew Passion* and painting your toenails an exotic purple would all be the reflex of economic forces. Any battle not fought for directly economic motives, or any work of art which is silent on the class struggle, would be inconceivable.

Marx himself occasionally writes as though the political is simply the reflex of the economic. Yet he also often investigates the social, political or military motives behind historical events, without the faintest suggestion that these motives are just the surface manifestations of deeper economic ones. Material forces do sometimes leave their mark quite directly on politics, art and social life. But their influence is generally more long-term and subterranean than this. There are times when this influence is only very partial, and other times when it scarcely makes sense to speak in these terms at all. How is the capitalist mode of production the cause of my taste in neckties? In what sense does it determine hang-gliding or the twelve-bar blues?

So there is no reductionism at work here. Politics, culture, science, ideas and social existence are not just economics in disguise, as some neuroscientists hold that the mind is just the brain in disguise. They have their own reality, evolve their own histories and operate by their own inner logic. They are not just the pale reflection of something else. They also powerfully shape the mode of production itself. The traffic between economic "base" and social "superstructure," as we shall see later, is not just one way. So if we are not speaking here of some mechanistic determinism, what kind of claim *is* being made? Is it one so fuzzy and generalized as to be politically toothless?

The claim is in the first place a negative one. It is that the way men and women produce their material life sets limits to the kind of cultural, legal, political and social institutions they construct. The word "determine" literally means "to set limits to." Modes of production do not dictate a specific kind of politics, culture or set of ideas. Capitalism was not the cause of John Locke's philosophy or Jane Austen's fiction. It is rather a context in which both can be illuminated. Nor do modes of production throw up only those ideas or institutions which serve their purposes. If this were true, then Marxism itself would be impossible. It would be a mystery where anarchist street theatre comes from, or how Tom Paine came to write one of the best-selling books of all time—the revolutionary *Rights of Man*—at the heart of the repressive police state that was the England of his day. Even so, we would be astonished to discover that English culture contained nothing but Tom Paines and anarchist theatre groups. Most novelists, scholars, advertisers, newspapers, teachers and television stations do not produce work that is dramatically subversive of the status quo. This is so glaringly obvious that it generally fails to strike us as significant. Marx's point is simply that it is not an accident. And it is here that we can formulate the more positive aspect of his claim. Broadly speaking, the culture, law and politics of class-society are bound up with the interests of the dominant social classes. As Marx himself puts it in *The German Ideology*, "The class that is the ruling *material* force of society is at the same time the ruling *intellectual* force."

Most people, if they pause to think about it, would probably accept that the business of material production has loomed so large in human history, absorbed such boundless resources of time and energy, provoked such internecine conflicts, engrossed so many human beings from cradle to grave and confronted so many of them as a matter of life or death, that it would be amazing if it were not to leave its mark on a good many other aspects of our existence. Other social institutions find themselves inexorably dragged into its orbit. It bends politics, law, culture and ideas out of true by demanding that rather than just flourish as themselves, they spend much of their time legitimating the prevailing social order. Think of contemporary capitalism, in which the commodity form has left its grubby thumbprints on everything from sport to sexuality, from how best to swing oneself a front-row seat in heaven to the ear-shattering tones in which U.S. television reporters hope to seize the viewer's attention for the sake of the advertisers. The most compelling confirmation of Marx's theory of history is late capitalist society. There is a sense in which his case is becoming truer as time passes. It is capitalism, not Marxism, which is economically reductionist. It is capitalism which believes in production for production's sake, in the narrower sense of the word "production."

Marx, by contrast, believes in production for its own sake in a more generous sense of the word. He argues that human self-realisation is to be valued as an end in itself, rather than reduced to the instrument of some other goal. This, he thought, would prove impossible as long as the narrower sense of production for production's sake prevailed— for then most of our creative energy would be invested in producing the means of living rather than savouring life itself. Much of the meaning of Marxism can be found in the contrast between these two uses of the phrase "production for production's sake"—one of them economic, the other creative or artistic. Far from being an economic reductionist, Marx is a stern critic of reducing human production to tractors and turbines. The production that mattered to him was closer to art than it was to assembling transistor radios or slaughtering sheep. We shall be returning to this subject in a moment.

It is true, even so, that Marx insists on the central role played by the economic (in the narrow sense of the word) in history to date. But this is far from a belief confined to Marxists. Cicero held that the purpose of the state was to protect private property. The "economic" theory of history was a commonplace of the eighteenth-century Enlightenment. A number of Enlightenment thinkers saw history as a succession of modes of production. They also believed that this could explain rank, lifestyles, social inequalities and relations within both family and government. Adam Smith regarded each stage of material development in history as generating its own forms of law, property and government. Jean-Jacques Rousseau argues in his *Discourse on Inequality* that property brings war, exploitation and class conflict in its wake. He also insists that the so-called social contract is a fraud perpetrated by the rich on the poor to protect their privileges. Rousseau speaks of human society fettering the weak and giving powers to the rich from the outset—powers that "irretrievably destroyed natural liberty, established for all time the law of property and inequality . . . and for the benefit of a few ambitious men subjected the human race thenceforth to labour, servitude and misery."[4] The law, Rousseau considers, generally backs the strong over the weak; justice is for the most part a weapon of violence and domination; and culture, science, the arts and religion are harnessed to the business of defending the status quo, flinging "garlands of flowers" over the chains which weigh men and women down. It is property, Rousseau claims, that lies at the root of human discontent.

The great nineteenth-century Irish economist John Elliot Cairnes, who regarded socialism as "a rank outgrowth of economic ignorance" and was once described as the most orthodox of all classical economists, observed "how extensively the material interests of men prevail in determining their political opinions and conduct."[5] He also remarked in the Preface to his book *The Slave Power* that "the course of history is largely determined by the action of economic causes." His compatriot W. E. H. Lecky, the greatest Irish historian of his day and a virulent antisocialist, wrote that "few things contribute so much to the formation of the social type as the laws regulating the succession of property."[6] Even Sigmund Freud clung to a form of economic determination. Without the need to labour, he considered, we would simply lie around the place all day shamelessly indulging our libidos. It was economic necessity which jolted us out of our natural indolence and prodded us into social activity.

Or take this little-known piece of historical materialist commentary:

> The inhabitant [of human society] must go through the different stages of hunter, shepherd, and husbandman, then when property becomes valuable, and consequently gives cause for injustice; then when laws are appointed to repress injury, and secure possession, when men by the sanction of these laws, become possessed of superfluity, when luxury is thus introduced and demands its continual supply, then it is that the sciences become necessary and useful; the state cannot subsist without them ...[7]

Not the reflections of a Marxist with a quaintly archaic prose style, but the ruminations of the eighteenth-century Irish writer Oliver Goldsmith, who was a devout Tory. If the Irish seem to have been particularly inclined to the so-called economic theory of history, it was because it was hard to live in such a down-at-heel colony, dominated as it was by the Anglo-Irish landowning class, and overlook such matters altogether. In England, with its complex cultural superstructure, economic issues were less painfully evident to poets and historians. Today, many of those who would scornfully reject Marx's theory of history behave for all the world as though it were true. These people are known as bankers, financial advisors, Treasury officials, corporate executives and the like. Everything they do testifies to their faith in the priority of the economic. They are spontaneous Marxists to a man.

It is worth adding that in a pleasing symmetry, the "economic theory of history" was born in and around Manchester, just as industrial capitalism was. It was his time in the city, Engels remarked, which first made him aware of the centrality of the economic. Since his father, as we have seen, ran a mill there which supported both Engels and (for much of the time) Marx himself, this insight, one might say, began at home. The well-heeled Engels acted as the material base to Marx's intellectual superstructure.

The claim that everything for Marx is determined by "economics" is an absurd oversimplification. What shapes the course of history in his view is class struggle; and classes are not reducible to economic factors. It is true that Marx sees classes for the most part as groups of men and women who occupy the same place within a mode of production. But it is significant that we speak of social classes, not of economic ones. Marx writes of the "social" relations of production, as well as of "social" revolution. If the social relations of production have priority over the forces of production, then it is hard to see how something baldly labelled "the economic" can be the prime mover of history.

Classes do not exist only in coal mines and insurance offices. They are also social formations, communities as much as economic entities. They involve customs, traditions, social institutions, sets of values and habits of thought. They are also political phenomena. In fact, there are hints in Marx's work that a class lacking political representation is not in the full sense a class at all. Classes, he seems to suggest, only truly become classes when they become conscious of themselves as such. They involve legal, social, cultural, political and ideological processes. In precapitalist societies, so Marx argues, these noneconomic factors are of especial importance. Classes are not uniform, but reveal a good deal of internal division and diversity.

Besides, as we shall see shortly, labour for Marx concerns a great deal more than the economic. It involves a whole anthropology—a theory of Nature and human agency, the body and its needs, the nature of the senses, ideas of social cooperation and individual self-fulfillment. This is not economics as the *Wall Street Journal* knows it. You do not read much about human-species-being in the *Financial Times*. Labour also involves gender, kinship and sexuality. There is the question of how labourers are produced in the first place, and of how they are materially sustained and spiritually replenished. Production is carried on within specific forms of life, and is thus suffused with social meaning. Because labour always signifies, humans being significant (literally, sign-making) animals, it can never be simply a technical or material affair. You may see it as a way of praising God, glorifying the Fatherland or acquiring your beer money. The economic, in short, always presupposes a lot more than itself. It is not just a matter of how the markets are behaving. It concerns the way we become human beings, not just the way we become stockbrokers.[8]

Classes, then, are not just economic, any more than sexuality is simply personal. In fact, it is hard to think of anything that is just economic. Even coins can be collected and displayed in glass cases, admired for their aesthetic qualities or melted down for their metal. To speak of money, incidentally, is to grasp why it is so easy to reduce the whole of human existence to the economic, since there is a sense in which this is exactly what money does. What is so magical about money is that it compresses such a wealth of human possibilities into its slim compass. It is true that there are a great many things in life more valuable than money, but it is money which gives us access to most of them. Money allows us to engage in fulfilling relationships with others without the social embarrassment of suddenly falling down dead of hunger. It can buy you privacy, health, education, beauty, social rank, mobility, comfort, freedom, respect and sensuous fulfillment, along with a Tudor grange in Warwickshire. Marx writes wonderfully in the *Economic and Philosophical Manuscripts* of the protean, shapechanging, alchemical nature of money, the way you can conjure such a dazzling array of goods from its unremarkable form. Money is itself a kind of reductionism. It packs whole universes into a handful of copper.

But even coins, as we have seen, are not raw economics. In fact, "the economy" never appears in the raw. What the financial press calls "the economy" is a kind of phantom. Certainly nobody has ever clapped eyes on it. It is an abstraction from a complex social process. It is orthodox economic thought which tends to narrow the notion of the economic. Marxism, by contrast, conceives of production in the richest, most capacious kind of way. One reason why Marx's theory of history holds good is the fact that material goods are never just material goods. They hold out the promise of human well-being. They are the portal to so much that is precious in human life. This is why men and women have struggled to the death over land, property, money and capital. Nobody values the economic simply as the economic, other than those who make a professional career out of it. It is because this realm of human existence folds so many other dimensions into itself that it plays such a key role in human history.

Marxism has often been accused of being a mirror image of its political opponents. Just as capitalism reduces humanity to Economic Man, so does its great antagonist. Capitalism makes a deity of material production, and Marx does just the same. But this is to misunderstand Marx's notion of production. Most of the production that goes on, he insists, is not true production at all. In his view, men and women only genuinely produce when they do so freely and for its own sake. Only under communism will this be fully possible; but meanwhile we can gain a foretaste of such creativity in the specialized form of production we know as art. John Milton, Marx writes, "produced *Paradise Lost* for the same reason that a silkworm produces silk. It was an activity of *his* nature."[9] Art is an image of nonalienated labour. It is how Marx liked to think of his own writings, which he once described as forming "an artistic whole" and which he penned (unlike most of his disciples) with a meticulous attention to style. Nor was his interest in art purely theoretical. He himself wrote lyric poetry, an unfinished comic novel, a fragment of verse drama and a sizeable unpublished manuscript on art and religion. He also planned a journal of dramatic criticism and a treatise of aesthetics. His knowledge of world literature was staggering in its scope.

Human labour has rarely been of a fulfilling kind. For one thing, it has always been coerced in one way or another, even if the coercion in question is simply the need not to starve. For another thing, it has been carried on in class-society, and thus not as an end in itself but as a means to the power and profit of others. For Marx, as for his mentor Aristotle, the good life consists of activities engaged in for their own sake. The best things are done just for the hell of it. We do them simply because they belong to our fulfillment as the kind of animals we are, not out of duty, custom, sentiment, authority, material necessity, social utility or fear of the Almighty. There is no reason, for example, why we should delight in one another's company. When we do so, however, we are realizing a vital capacity of our "species being." And this in Marx's view is as much a form of production as planting potatoes. Human solidarity is essential for the purpose of political change; but in the end it serves as its own reason. So much is clear from a moving passage in the *Economic and Philosophical Manuscripts*:

> When communist workmen gather together, their immediate aim is instruction, propaganda, etc. But at the same time they acquire a new need—a need for society—and what appears as a means has be-

come an end. Smoking, eating and drinking, etc, are no longer means of creating links between people. Company, association, conversation, which in its turn has society as its goal, is enough for them. The brotherhood of man is not a hollow phrase, it is a reality, and the nobility of man shines forth upon us from their work-worn figures.[10]

Production for Marx, then, means realizing one's essential powers in the act of transforming reality. True wealth, he claims in the *Grundrisse,* is "the absolute working-out of human creative potentialities . . . i.e. the development of all human powers as an end in itself, not as measured on a predetermined yardstick."[11] Beyond class-history, he writes in *Capital,* can begin "that development of human energy which is an end in itself, the true realm of freedom."[12] The word "production" in Marx's work covers any self-fulfilling activity: playing the flute, savouring a peach, wrangling over Plato, dancing a reel, making a speech, engaging in politics, organising a birthday party for one's children. It has no muscular, macho implications. When Marx speaks of production as the essence of humanity, he does not mean that the essence of humanity is packing sausages. Labour as we know it is an alienated form of what he calls "praxis"—an ancient Greek word meaning the kind of free, self-realising activity by which we transform the world. In ancient Greece, the word meant any activity of a free man, as opposed to a slave.

Yet only the economic in the narrow sense will allow us to get beyond the economic. By redeploying the resources capitalism has so considerately stored up for us, socialism can allow the economic to take more of a backseat. It will not evaporate, but it will become less obtrusive. To enjoy a sufficiency of goods means not to have to think about money all the time. It frees us for less tedious pursuits. Far from being obsessed with economic matters, Marx saw them as a travesty of true human potential. He wanted a society where the economic no longer monopolised so much time and energy.

That our ancestors should have been so preoccupied with material matters is understandable. Where you can produce only a slim economic surplus, or scarcely any surplus at all, you will perish without ceaseless hard labour. Capitalism, however, generates the sort of surplus that really could be used to increase leisure on a sizeable scale. The irony is that it creates this wealth in a way that demands constant accumulation and expansion, and thus constant labour. It also creates it in ways that generate poverty and hardship. It is a self-thwarting system. As a result, modern men and women, surrounded by an affluence unimaginable to hunter-gatherers, ancient slaves or feudal serfs, end up working as long and hard as ever these predecessors did.

Marx's work is all about human enjoyment. The good life for him is not one of labour but of leisure. Free self-realisation is a form of "production," to be sure; but it is not one that is coercive. And leisure is necessary if men and women are to devote time to running their own affairs. It is thus surprising that Marxism does not attract more card-carrying idlers and professional loafers to its ranks. This, however, is because a lot of energy must be expended on achieving this goal. Leisure is something you have to work for.

SIX

Marx was a materialist. He believed that nothing exists but matter. He had no interest in the spiritual aspects of humanity, and saw human consciousness as just a reflex of the material world. He was brutally dismissive of religion, and regarded morality simply as a question of the end justifying the means. Marxism drains humanity of all that is most precious about it, reducing us to inert lumps of material stuff determined by our environment. There is an obvious route from this dreary, soulless vision of humanity to the atrocities of Stalin and other disciples of Marx.

Whether the world is made of matter, spirit or green cheese is not a question over which Marx lost much sleep. He was disdainful of such large metaphysical abstractions, and had a brisk way of dispatching them as idly speculative. As one of the most formidable minds of modernity, Marx was notably allergic to fancy ideas. Those who regard him as a bloodless theorist forget that he was among other things a Romantic thinker with a suspicion of the abstract and a passion for the concrete and specific. The abstract, he thought, was simple and featureless; it was the concrete that was rich and complex. So whatever materialism meant to him, it certainly did not revolve on the question of what the world was made out of.

This, among other things, was what it meant to the materialist philosophers of the eighteenth-century Enlightenment, some of whom saw human beings as mere mechanical functions of the material world. Marx himself, however, regarded this kind of thought as thoroughly ideological. For one thing, it reduced men and women to a passive condition. Their minds were seen as blank sheets, on which they received sensory impressions from the material world outside. And out of these impressions they formed their ideas. So if these impressions could somehow be manipulated to produce the "right" kind of ideas, human beings could make steady progress towards a state of social perfection. This was not a politically innocent affair. The ideas in question were those of an elite of middle-class thinkers who were champions of individualism, private property and the free market as well as justice, liberty and human rights. Through this mind-altering process, they hoped in a paternal sort of way to influence the behavior of the common people. It is hard to believe that Marx subscribed to *this* kind of materialism.

This is not all that materialist philosophy meant before Marx got his hands on it. In one way or another, however, he saw it as a form of thought closely bound up with the fortunes of the middle classes. His own brand of materialism, as developed in his *Theses on Feuerbach* and elsewhere, was quite different, and Marx was fully conscious of the fact. He was aware that he was breaking with an old style of materialism and originating something quite new. Materialism for Marx meant starting from what human beings actually were, rather than from some shadowy ideal to which we could aspire. And what we were was in the first place a species of practical, material, bodily beings. Anything else we were, or could be, had to be derived from this fundamental fact.

In a boldly innovative move, Marx rejected the passive human subject of middle-class materialism and put in its place an active one. All philosophy had to start from the premise that whatever else they were, men and women were first of all *agents*. They were creatures who transformed themselves in the act of transforming their material surroundings. They were not the pawns of History or Matter or Spirit, but active, self-determining beings who were capable of making their own history. And this means that the Marxist version of materialism is a democratic one, in contrast to the intellectual elitism of the Enlightenment. Only through the collective practical activity of the majority of people can the ideas which govern our lives be really changed. And this is because these ideas are deeply embedded in our actual behavior.

In this sense, Marx was more of an antiphilosopher than a philosopher. In fact, Etienne Balibar has called him "perhaps . . . the greatest antiphilosopher of the modern age."[1]

TERRY EAGLETON

Antiphilosophers are those who are wary of philosophy—not just in the sense that Brad Pitt might be, but nervous of it for philosophically interesting reasons. They tend to come up with ideas that are suspicious of ideas; and though they are for the most part entirely rational, they tend not to believe that reason is what it all comes down to. Feuerbach, from whom Marx learned some of his materialism, wrote that any authentic philosophy has to begin with its opposite, nonphilosophy. The philosopher, he remarked, must accept "what in man does *not* philosophise, what is rather opposed to philosophy and abstract thought."[2] He also commented that "it is *man* who thinks, not the Ego or Reason."[3] As Alfred Schmidt observes, "The understanding of man as a needy, sensuous, physiological being is therefore the precondition of any theory of subjectivity."[4] Human consciousness, in other words, is corporeal—which is not to say that it is nothing more than the body. It is rather a sign of the way in which the body is always in a sense unfinished, open-ended, always capable of more creative activity than what it may be manifesting right now.

We think as we do, then, because of the kind of animals we are. If our thought is strung out in time, it is because that is the way our bodies and sense-perceptions are too. Philosophers sometimes wonder whether a machine could think. Maybe it could, but it would be in a way very different from ourselves. This is because a machine's material makeup is so different from ours. It has no bodily needs, for example, and none of the emotional life which in the case of us humans is bound up with such needs. Our own kind of thinking is inseparable from this sensory, practical and emotional context. This is why, if a machine could think, we might not be able to understand what it was thinking.

The philosophy Marx broke with was for the most part a contemplative affair. Its typical scenario was that of a passive, isolated, disembodied human subject disinterestedly surveying an isolated object. Marx, as we have seen, rejected this kind of subject; but he also insisted that the object of our knowledge is not something eternally fixed and given. It is more likely to be the product of our own historical activity. Just as we have to rethink the subject as a form of practice, so we have to rethink the objective world as the result of human practice. And this means among other things that it can in principle be changed.

Starting with human beings as active and practical, and then situating their thought within that context, help us to cast new light on some of the problems which have plagued philosophers. People who work on the world are less likely to doubt that there is anything out there than those who contemplate it from a leisurely distance. In fact, sceptics can exist in the first place only because there is something out there. If there were not a material world to feed them they would die, and their doubts would perish along with them. If you believe that human beings are passive in the face of reality, this may also persuade you to query the existence of such a world. This is because we confirm the existence of things by experiencing their resistance to our demands. And we do this primarily through our practical activity.

Philosophers have sometimes raised the question of "other minds." How do we know that the human bodies we encounter have minds like ours? A materialist would reply that if they did not, we would probably not be around to raise the question. There could be no material production to keep us alive without social cooperation, and the capacity to communicate with others is a large part of what we mean by having a mind. One might also point out that the word "mind" is a way of describing the behavior of a particular kind of body: a creative, meaningful, communicative one. We do not need to peer inside people's heads or wire them up to machines to see whether they possess this mysterious entity. We look at what they do. Consciousness is not some spectral phenomenon; it is something we can see, hear and handle. Human bodies are lumps of material, but peculiarly creative, expressive ones; and it is this creativity that we call "mind." To call human beings rational is to say that their behavior reveals a pattern of meaning or significance. Enlightenment materialists have sometimes been rightly accused of reducing the world to so much dead, meaningless matter. Just the reverse is true of Marx's materialism.

Why Marx Was Right

The materialist's response to the sceptic is not a knock-down argument. You might always claim that our experience of social cooperation, or of the world's resistance to our projects, is itself not to be trusted. Perhaps we are only imagining these things. But looking at such problems in a materialist spirit can illuminate them in a new way. It is possible to see, for example, how intellectuals who begin from the disembodied mind, and quite often end up there as well, are likely to be puzzled by how the mind relates to the body, as well as to the bodies of others. It may be that they see a gap between mind and world. This is ironic, since it is quite often the way the world shapes their own minds that gives rise to this idea. Intellectuals themselves are a caste of people somewhat remote from the material world. Only on the back of a material surplus in society is it possible to produce a professional elite of priests, sages, artists, counsellors, Oxford dons and the like.

Plato thought that philosophy required a leisured aristocratic elite. You cannot have literary salons and learned societies if everyone has to work just to keep social life ticking over. Ivory towers are as rare as bowling alleys in tribal cultures. (They are just as rare in advanced societies, where universities have become organs of corporate capitalism.) Because intellectuals do not need to labour in the sense that bricklayers do, they can come to regard themselves and their ideas as independent of the rest of social existence. And this is one of the many things that Marxists mean by ideology. Such people tend not to see that their very distance from society is itself socially conditioned. The prejudice that thought is independent of reality is itself shaped by social reality.

For Marx, our thought takes shape in the process of working on the world, and this is a material necessity determined by our bodily needs. One might claim, then, that thinking itself is a material necessity. Thinking and our bodily drives are closely related, as they are for Nietzsche and Freud. Consciousness is the result of an interaction between ourselves and our material surroundings. It is itself a historical product. Humanity, Marx writes, is "established" by the material world, since only by engaging with it can we exercise our powers and have their reality confirmed. It is the "otherness" of reality, its resistance to our designs on it, which first brings us to self-awareness. And this means above all the existence of others. It is through others that we become what we are. Personal identity is a social product. There could not just be one person, any more than there could just be one number.

At the same time, however, this reality should be recognized as the work of our own hands. Not to see it as this—to regard it as something natural or inexplicable, independent of our own activity—is what Marx calls alienation. He means the condition in which we forget that history is our own production, and come to be mastered by it as by an alien force. For

Marx, writes the German philosopher Jürgen Habermas, the objectivity of the world "is grounded ... in the bodily organisation of human beings, which is oriented towards action."[5]

In a sense, then, consciousness is always in some sense "belated," as reason is belated in a child. Before we even come to reflect, we are always already situated in a material context; and our thought, however apparently abstract and theoretical, is shaped to the core by this fact. It is philosophical idealism which forgets that our ideas have a foundation in practice. By detaching them from this context, it can fall victim to the illusion that it is thought which creates reality.

So there is a close link for Marx between our reasoning and our bodily life. The human senses represent a kind of borderline between the two. For some idealist philosophers, by contrast, "matter" is one thing and ideas or "spirit" quite another. For Marx, the human body is itself a refutation of this split. More precisely, it is the human body in action which refutes it. For that practice is clearly a material affair; but it is also, inseparably, a matter of meanings, values, purposes and intentions. If it is "subjective," it is also "objective." Or perhaps it throws that whole distinction into question. Some previous thinkers had seen the mind as active and the senses as passive. Marx, however, sees the human senses as themselves forms of active engagement with reality. They are the result of a long history of interaction with the material world. "The cultivation of the five senses," he writes in the

Economic and Philosophical Manuscripts, "is the work of all previous history."

A thinker like Locke or Hume starts with the senses; Marx, by contrast, asks where the senses themselves come from. And the answer goes something like this. Our biological needs are the foundation of history. We have a history because we are creatures of lack, and in that sense history is natural to us. Nature and history are in Marx's view sides of the same coin. As our needs get caught up in history, however, they undergo transformation. In satisfying certain needs, for example, we find ourselves creating new ones. And in this whole process, our sensory life is shaped and refined. All this comes about because the satisfaction of our needs also involves desire, but it was left to Freud to fill in this part of the picture.

In this way, we begin to tell a story. In fact, we begin to *be* a story. Animals that are not capable of desire, complex labour and elaborate forms of communication tend to repeat themselves. Their lives are determined by natural cycles. They do not shape a narrative for themselves, which is what Marx knows as freedom. The irony in his view is that though this self-determination is of the essence of humanity, the great majority of men and women throughout history have been unable to exercise it. They have not been permitted to be fully human. Instead, their lives have been for the most part determined by the dreary cycles of class-society. Why this has been so, and how it can be put right, is what Marx's work is all about. It is about how we might move from the kingdom of necessity to the realm of freedom. This means becoming rather less like badgers and rather more like ourselves. And having brought us to the threshold of that freedom, Marx leaves us there to fend for ourselves. How could it be freedom otherwise?

If you want to avoid the dualisms of the philosophers, then, just look at how human beings actually behave. A human body is in one sense a material object, part of Nature as well as part of history. Yet it is a peculiar kind of object, quite unlike cabbages and coal scuttles. For one thing, it has the capacity to change its situation. It can also turn Nature into a kind of extension of itself, which is not true of coal scuttles. Human labour works Nature up into that extension of our bodies which we know as civilisation. All human institutions, from art galleries and opium dens to casinos and the World Health Organisation, are extensions of the productive body.

They are also embodiments of human consciousness. "Human industry," Marx writes, using the word "industry" in the broadest possible sense, "is the open book of human consciousness, human psychology perceived in sensory terms."[6] The body can do all this because it has the power to transcend itself—to transform itself and its situation, as well as to enter into complex relationships with other bodies of its kind, in that open-ended process we know as history. Human bodies which cannot do this are known as corpses.

Cabbages cannot do this either, but neither do they need to. They are purely natural entities, without the sorts of needs we find in humans. Humans can make history because of the kind of productive creatures they are; but they also need to do so, because in conditions of scarcity they have to keep producing and reproducing their material life. It is this which prods them into constant activity. They have a history out of necessity. In a situation of material abundance, we would still have a history, but in a different sense of the word from the one we have known so far. We can fulfill our natural needs only by social means—by collectively producing our means of production. And this then gives rise to other needs, which in turn gives rise to others. But at the root of all this, which we know as culture, history or civilisation, lies the needy human body and its material conditions. This is just another way of saying that the economic is the foundation of our life together. It is the vital link between the biological and the social.

This, then, is how we come to have history; but it is also what we mean by spirit. Spiritual matters are not disembodied, otherworldly affairs. It is the prosperous bourgeois who tends to see spiritual questions as a realm loftily remote from everyday life, since he needs a hiding place from his own crass materialism. It comes as no surprise that material girls like Madonna should be so fascinated by Kabbala. For

Marx, by contrast, "spirit" is a question of art, friendship, fun, compassion, laughter, sexual love, rebellion, creativity, sensuous delight, righteous anger and abundance of life. (He did, however, sometimes take the fun a bit too far: he once went on a pub crawl from Oxford Street to Hampstead Road with a couple of friends, stopping at every pub en route, and was chased by the police for throwing paving stones at street lamps.[7] His theory of the repressive nature of the state, so it would seem, was no mere abstract speculation). In *The Eighteenth Brumaire of Louis Bonaparte,* he discusses politics in terms of social interests, as one might expect; but he also writes eloquently of politics as expressing "old memories, personal enmities, fears and hopes, prejudices and illusions, sympathies and antipathies, convictions, articles of faith and principles." And all this from the bloodlessly clinical thinker of anti-Marxist fantasy.

All of the spiritual activities I have just listed are bound up with the body, since that is the kind of beings we are. Anything which doesn't involve my body doesn't involve me. When I speak to you on the phone I am present to you bodily, though not physically. If you want an image of the soul, remarked the philosopher Ludwig Wittgenstein, look at the human body. Happiness for Marx, as for Aristotle, was a practical activity, not a state of mind. For the Judaic tradition of which he was an unbelieving offspring, the "spiritual" is a question of feeding the hungry, welcoming the immigrants and protecting the poor from the violence of the rich. It is not the opposite of mundane, everyday existence. It is a particular way of living it.

There is one activity of the body in which "spirit" is made particularly manifest, and that is language. Like the body as a whole, language is the material embodiment of spirit or human consciousness. "Language," Marx writes in *The German Ideology,* "is as old as consciousness, language *is* practical, real consciousness that exists for other men as well, and only therefore does it exist for me; language, like consciousness, only arises from the need, the necessity, of intercourse with other men."[8] Consciousness is social and practical through and through, which is why language is the supreme sign of it. I can be said to have a mind only because I am born into a shared heritage of meaning. Marx also speaks of language as "the communal being speaking for itself." The language of philosophy, he remarks, is a distorted version of the language of the actual world. Thought and language, far from existing in a sphere of their own, are manifestations of actual life. Even the most rarefied concepts can be traced back eventually to our common existence.

Human consciousness, then, requires a great deal of material stage-setting. And to start from human consciousness, as so much philosophy does, is generally to ignore this fact. It is to beg too many questions.[9] Conventional philosophy does not start far back enough. It overlooks the social conditions which put ideas in place, the passions with which they are involved, the power struggles with which they are entangled, the material needs they serve. It does not typically ask "Where did this human subject come from?," or "How did the object come to be produced?" Before we can think, we have to eat; and the word "eat" opens up the question of a whole mode of social production. We also have to be born; and the word "born" opens up the whole domain of kinship, sexuality, patriarchy, sexual reproduction and so on. Before we come to reflect on reality, we are already bound up with it practically and emotionally, and our thinking always goes on within this context. As the philosopher John Macmurray comments, "Our knowledge of the world is primarily an aspect of our action in the world."[10] "Men," Marx writes in Heideggerian vein in his *Comments on Wagner,* "do not in any way begin by finding themselves in a theoretical relationship to the things of the external world."[11] A lot has to be in place before we can start to reason.

Our thought is bound up with the world in another sense, too. It is not just a "reflection" of reality, but a material force in its own right. Marxist theory itself is not just a commentary on the world, but an instrument for changing it. Marx himself occasionally talks as though thought were a mere "reflex" of material situations, but this fails to do justice to his own more subtle insights. Certain kinds of theory— emancipatory theories, as they are generally known—can act as a political force within the world, not just as a way of interpreting it. And this lends them a peculiar sort of feature. It means that they form a link between how things are and how they might be. They provide descriptions of how the world is; but in doing so they can help change the way men and women understand it, which in turn can play a part in changing reality. A slave knows he is a slave, but knowing why he is a slave is the first step towards not being one. So in portraying things as they are, such theories also offer a way of moving beyond them to a more desirable state of affairs. They step from how it is with them to how it ought to be. Theories of this kind allow men and women to describe themselves and their situations in ways that put them into question, and therefore eventually allow them to redescribe themselves. In this sense, there is a close relationship between reason, knowledge and freedom. Certain kinds of knowledge are vital for human freedom and happiness. And as people act on such knowledge, they come to grasp it more deeply, which then allows them to act on it more effectively. The more we can understand, the more we can do; but in Marx's view the kind of understanding that really matters can come about only through practical struggle. Just as playing the tuba is a form of practical knowledge, so is political emancipation.

It is for this reason that one must take Marx's celebrated eleventh thesis on Feuerbach with a pinch of salt. The philosophers, he writes there, have only interpreted the world;

the point is to change it. But how could you change the world without interpreting it? And isn't the power to interpret it in a particular light the beginnings of political change?

"It is social being," Marx writes in *The German Ideology,* "which determines consciousness." Or as Ludwig Wittgenstein put the point in his work *On Certainty:* "It is what we do which lies at the bottom of our language games."[12] This has important political consequences. It means, for example, that if we want to change the way we think and feel radically enough, we have to change what we do. Education or a change of heart are not enough. Our social being sets limits to our thought. And we could only break beyond these limits by changing that social being—which is to say, our material form of life. We could not get beyond the limits of our thought simply by taking thought.

But doesn't this involve a false dichotomy? If by "social being" we mean the kinds of things we do, then this must already involve consciousness. It is not as though consciousness lies on one side of a divide, and our social activities on the other. You cannot vote, kiss, shake hands or exploit migrant labour without meanings and intentions. We would not call a piece of behavior from which these things were absent a human action, any more than we would call tripping over a step or a rumbling in the gut a purposeful project. Marx would not, I think, deny this fact. As we have seen, he sees human consciousness as *embodied*—as incarnate in our practical behavior. Even so, he still holds that material existence is in some sense more fundamental than meanings and ideas, and that meanings and ideas can be explained in terms of it. How are we to make sense of this claim?

One answer, as we have seen already, is that thinking for humans is a material necessity, as it is in a more rudimentary way for beavers and hedgehogs. We need to think because of the kind of material animals we are. We are cognitive beings because we are corporeal ones. Cognitive procedures for Marx grow hand in hand with labour, industry and experiment. "The production of ideas, of conceptions, of consciousness," he writes in *The German Ideology,* "is at first directly interwoven with the material activity and the material intercourse of men, the language of real life."[13] If Nature simply dropped its luscious treasures into our gratefully gaping mouths, or if (perish the thought) we only needed to eat once in a lifetime, we might not have to do much thinking at all. Instead, we could just lie back and enjoy ourselves. But Nature, alas, is a good deal more niggardly than this, and the human body is racked by wants it must perpetually satisfy.

To begin with, then, it is our bodily needs which shape our way of thinking. And this is one sense in which thought is not paramount, even though a lot of thought likes to think it is. At a later stage of human development, Marx argues, ideas become much more independent of these needs, and this is what we know as culture. We can begin to relish ideas for their own sake, not for their survival value. Thought, as Bertolt Brecht once remarked, can become a real sensuous pleasure. Even so, it remains true that reasoning, however elevated, has its humble origins in biological need. As Friedrich Nietzsche taught, it is bound up with our exercise of power over Nature.[14] The drive to practical control of our environment, which is a life-or-death affair, underlies all our more abstract intellectual activity.

In this sense, there is something carnivalesque about the thought of Marx, as there is about the ideas of Nietzsche and Freud. The low is always a shadowy presence lurking within the high. As the critic William Empson remarks, "The most refined desires are inherent in the plainest, and would be false if they weren't."[15] At the root of our most lofty conceptions lie violence, lack, desire, appetite, scarcity and aggression. It is this which is the secret underside of what we call civilisation. Theodor Adorno speaks in graphic phrase of "the horror teeming under the stone of culture."[16] "The class struggle," writes Walter Benjamin, " . . . is a fight for the crude and material things without which no refined and spiritual things could exist."[17] We should note that Benjamin is not out to deny the value of "refined and spiritual things," any more than Marx is. He is concerned to put them in historical context. Like many a carnivalesque philosopher, Marx is a giant of a thinker with a heartfelt distrust of exalted ideas. Conventional politicians, by contrast, tend to speak publicly in earnestly idealist terms and talk privately in cynically materialist ones.

We have already touched on another sense in which "social being" has the edge over consciousness. This is the fact that the sort of understandings that really stick usually arise from what we actually do. In fact, social theorists speak of a kind of knowledge—tacit knowledge, they call it—which can *only* be acquired in the act of doing something, and which therefore cannot be handed on to someone else in theoretical form. Try explaining to someone how to whistle "Danny Boy." But even when our knowledge is not of this kind, the point remains valid. You could not learn how to play the violin from a teach-yourself book, then grab the instrument and dash off a dazzling rendition of Mendelssohn's Violin Concerto in E Minor. There is a sense in which one's knowledge of the concerto is inseparable from the capacity to perform it.

There is another sense in which material reality has the edge over ideas. When Marx speaks of consciousness, he is not always thinking of the ideas and values which are implicit in our daily activities. He is sometimes thinking of more formal systems of concepts such as law, science, politics and the like. And his point is that these forms of thought are ultimately determined by social reality. This, in fact, is the famous, much reviled Marxist doctrine of base and superstructure, which Marx outlines as follows:

> In the social production of their existence, men invariably enter into definite relations which are independent of their will, namely relations of production appropriate to a given stage in the development of the material forces of production. The totality of these relations of production constitutes the economic structure of society, the real foundation on which arises a legal and political superstructure, and to which correspond definite forms of social consciousness.[18]

By the "economic structure" or "base," Marx means the forces and relations of production; by the superstructure, he means institutions like the state, law, politics, religion and culture. In his view, the function of these institutions is to support the "base," meaning the prevailing class-system. Some of them, like culture and religion, perform this task largely by producing ideas which legitimate the system. This is known as ideology. "The ideas of the ruling class," Marx writes in *The German Ideology,* "are in every epoch the ruling ideas." It would be odd to come across a thriving feudal society in which most of the ideas in circulation were vehemently antifeudalist. As we have seen, Marx thought that those who controlled material production tended to control mental production as well.

TERRY EAGLETON

The claim has even more force in an age of press magnates and media barons than it had in his own time.

Since the base-superstructure model has been much derided by some of Marx's critics, and even by some of his adherents, I will perversely put in a good word for it here. It is sometimes objected that the model is too static; but all models are static, as well as simplifying. Marx does not mean that there are two entirely distinct slices to social life. On the contrary, there is a good deal of traffic between the two. The base may give rise to the superstructure, but the superstructure is important for the base's continued existence. Without the support of the state, the legal system, political parties and the circulation of pro-capitalist ideas in the media and elsewhere, the current property system might be somewhat more shaky than it is. In Marx's view, this two-way traffic was even more evident in precapitalist societies, where law, religion, politics, kinship and the state entered crucially into the business of material production.

Nor is the superstructure secondary to the base in the sense of being somehow less real. Prisons, churches, schools and television stations are every bit as real as banks and coal mines. Perhaps the base is more important than the superstructure; but more important from what viewpoint? Art is more important for the spiritual well-being of humanity than the invention of a new chocolate bar, but the latter is usually seen as part of the base while the former is not. The base is more important, Marxists would argue, in the sense that truly epoch-making changes in history are largely the result of material forces, not of ideas or beliefs.

Ideas and beliefs can be formidably influential; but the materialist claim is that they take on truly historic force only when they are allied with powerful material interests. Homer may see the Trojan war in terms of honour, valour, divine providence and the like, but the ancient Greek historian Thucydides, a full-blooded materialist in his own way, soberly points out that it was a shortage of resources, along with the Greeks' habit of breaking off warfare to embark on land cultivation and plundering expeditions, which spun out the conflict for so long. Thucydides also sees the whole system of Hellenic power as based on the development of navigation, and the commerce and accumulation that this enabled. Materialist theories of history stretch back long before Marx.

There are also a fair number of institutions which might be said to belong to both base and superstructure at the same time. Born-again churches in the United States are powerhouses of ideology but also immensely lucrative businesses. The same is true of publishing, the media and the film industry. Some U.S. universities are massive business enterprises as well as knowledge factories. Or think of Prince Charles, who exists largely to inspire deference in the British public, but who also makes a sizeable profit out of doing so.

But surely the whole of human existence cannot be

carved up between base and superstructure? Indeed not. There are countless things that belong neither to material production nor to the so-called superstructure. Language, sexual love, the tibia bone, the planet Venus, bitter remorse, dancing the tango and the North Yorkshire moors are just a few of them. Marxism, as we have seen, is not a Theory of Everything. It is true that one can stumble on the most improbable connections between class struggle and culture. Sexual love is relevant to the material base, since it quite often leads to the production of those potential new sources of labour power known as children. Dentists during the economic recession of 2008 reported a notable increase in jaw pains, brought on by teeth-gritting caused by stress. Clenching one's teeth in the face of catastrophe is apparently no longer a metaphor. When the novelist Marcel Proust was still in the womb, his genteel mother was greatly distressed by the outbreak of the socialistic Paris Commune; and some speculate that this distress was the cause of Proust's lifelong asthma. There is also a theory that Proust's immensely long, sinuous sentences are a kind of psychological compensation for his breathlessness. In which case there is a relation between Proust's syntax and the Paris Commune.

If the model suggests that the superstructure actually came into existence to serve the functions it does, then it is surely mistaken. This may be true of the state, but it is hardly true of art. Nor is it true to say that all the activities of schools, newspapers, churches and the state support the present social system. When schools teach infants how to tie their shoelaces, or television stations broadcast weather forecasts, there is no sense in which they are behaving "superstructurally." They are not buttressing the relations of production. The state sends its special forces to club peace demonstrators, but the police also search for missing children. When tabloid newspapers denounce immigrants, they are acting "super-structurally"; when they report road accidents they are most likely not. (Reports of road accidents, however, may always be used *against* the system. It is said that in the newsroom of the *Daily Worker,* the old British Communist Party newspaper, sub-editors would be handed reports of road accidents with the instruction "Class-angle that, comrade"). So to announce that schools, churches or TV stations belong to the super-structure is misleading. We may think of the superstructure less as a place than as a set of practices. Marx himself probably did not think of the superstructure in this way, but it is a useful refinement of his argument.

It is probably true that anything can in principle be used to prop up the current system. If the TV weatherman makes light of an approaching tornado because the news might de-press viewers, and listless citizens are unlikely to work as hard as cheerful ones, he is acting as an agent of the ruling powers. (There is a curious belief that gloom is politically subversive, not least in the pathologically upbeat United States.) In general, however, we might say that some aspects of these institutions behave in this way, and some do not. Or some may behave like this at some times and not at others. In which case an institution can be "superstructural" on Wednesday but not on Friday. The word "superstructure" invites us to put a practice in a specific kind of context. It is a relational term, asking what function one kind of activity serves in relation to another. As G. A. Cohen argues, it explains certain non-economic institutions in terms of the economic.[19] But it does not explain all such institutions, or all of what they get up to, or why they came into existence in the first place.

Even so, Marx's point is a sharper one than that suggests. It is not just a question of declaring that some things are superstructural and some are not, as some apples are russet and some are not. It is rather that if we examine the law, politics, religion, education and culture of class-societies, we will find that most of what they do lends support to the prevailing social order. And this, indeed, is no more than we should expect. There is no capitalist civilisation in which the law forbids private property, or in which children are regularly instructed in the evils of economic competition. It is true that a great deal of art and literature has been profoundly critical of the status quo. There is no sense in which Shelley, Blake, Mary Wollstonecraft, Emily Brontë, Dickens, George Orwell and D. H. Lawrence were all shamelessly pumping out propaganda on behalf of the ruling class. Yet if we look at

English literature as a whole, we find that its critique of the social order rarely extends to questioning the property system. In *Theories of Surplus Value* Marx speaks of what he calls "free spiritual production," under which he places art, as opposed to the production of ideology. It might be more accurate to say that art encompasses both.

In Thomas Hardy's novel *Jude the Obscure*, Jude Fawley, an impoverished artisan living in the working-class area of Oxford known as Jericho, reflects that his destiny lies not with the spires and quadrangles of the university, but "among the manual toilers in the shabby purlieu which he himself occupied, unrecognized as part of the city at all by its visitors and panegyrists, yet without whose denizens the hard readers could not read nor the high thinkers live" (Part 2, Ch. 6). Are these poignant words a statement of Marx's base/superstructure doctrine? Not exactly. In materialist spirit, they draw attention to the fact that there can be no mental labour without manual labour. Oxford University is the "superstructure" to Jericho's "base." If the academics had to be their own cooks, plumbers, stone masons, printers and so on, they would have no time to study. Every work of philosophy presupposes an obscure army of manual labourers, just as every symphony and cathedral does. But Marx means more than this, as we have seen already. It is not just that in order to study Plato you have to eat. It is also that the way material production is organised will tend to affect the way you think about him.

It is the nature of the thinking carried on in Oxford, not just the fact that thinking goes on there at all, which is the point at stake. Like anyone else, Oxford academics find their thought shaped by the material realities of their age. Most of them are unlikely to interpret Plato, or for that matter any other writer, in a way which undermines the rights of private property, the need for social order and so on. When Jude writes a desperate note to the Master of one of the colleges asking how he might become a student there, he receives back a note suggesting that a working man like himself would be better off not trying. (The irony is that Hardy himself probably agrees with this advice, though not with the reasons for which it was given.)

Why should there be a need for superstructures in the first place? This, note, is a different question from asking why we have art or law or religion. There are many answers to that. It is asking, rather, "Why should so much art, law and religion act to legitimate the present system?" The answer, in a word, is that the "base" is self-divided. Because it involves exploitation, it gives rise to a good deal of conflict. And the role of superstructures is to regulate and ratify those conflicts. Superstructures are essential because exploitation exists. If it did not, we would still have art, law and perhaps even religion. But they would no longer serve these disreputable functions. Instead, they could throw off these constraints and be all the freer for it.

Why Marx Was Right

155

The base-superstructure model is a vertical one. Yet one can also think of it horizontally. If we do, the base can be seen as the outer limit of political possibility. It is what ultimately resists our demands—what refuses to yield even when every other kind of reform has been conceded. The model thus has a political importance. Someone who supposed that you could change the fundamentals of society simply by changing people's ideas or launching a new political party might find it instructive to be shown how these things, while often of key significance, are not what men and women ultimately live by. He might accordingly redirect his energies to some more fruitful goal. The base represents the final obstacle against which a socialist politics continually presses up. It is, as Americans say, the bottom line. And since by the bottom line Americans sometimes mean money, this just goes to show how many citizens in the Land of the Free are unwitting Marxists. That this is so became obvious to me some years ago, when I was driving with the Dean of Arts of a state university in the American Midwest past thickly blooming cornfields. Casting a glance at this rich crop, he remarked "The harvest should be good this year. Might just get a couple of assistant professorships out of that."

Materialists, then, are not soulless creatures. Or if they are, it is not necessarily because they are materialists. Marx himself was a formidably cultivated man in the great central European tradition, who longed to be finished with what he scathingly called the "economic crap" of *Capital* in order to write his big book on Balzac. Unluckily for him, but perhaps fortunately for us, he never did. He once remarked that he had sacrificed his health, happiness and family to writing *Capital,* but that he would have been an "ox" if he had turned his back on the sufferings of humankind.[20] He also observed that nobody had written so much on money and had so little. As a man, he was passionate, satirical and humorous, an indomitable spirit full of gusto, geniality and ferocious polemic who stubbornly survived both dire poverty and chronic ill health.[21] He was, of course, an atheist; but one does not need to be religious to be spiritual, and some of the great themes of Judaism —justice, emancipation, the reign of peace and plenty, the day of reckoning, history as a narrative of liberation, the redemption not just of the individual but of a whole dispossessed people—inform his work in suitably secularised form. He also inherited the Jewish hostility to idols, fetishes and enslaving illusions.

As far as religion goes, it is worth pointing out that there have been Jewish Marxists, Islamic Marxists, and Christian Marxists who champion so-called liberation theology. All of them are materialists in Marx's sense of the word. In fact, Eleanor Marx, Marx's daughter, reports that Marx once told her mother that if she wanted "satisfaction of her metaphysical needs" she should find them in the Jewish prophets rather than in the Secular Society she sometimes attended.[22] Marxist materialism is not a set of statements about the cosmos, such as "Everything is made out of atoms" or "There is no God." It is a theory of how historical animals function.

In line with his Judaic legacy, Marx was a strenuously moral thinker. If he intended to write a book on Balzac after finishing *Capital,* he also proposed to write one on ethics. So much, then, for the prejudice that he was a bloodless amoralist whose approach to society was purely scientific. It is hard to feel this of a man who writes that capitalist society "has torn up all genuine bonds between men and replaced them by selfishness, selfish need, and dissolved the world of men into a world of atomized individuals, hostile towards each other."[23] Marx believed that the ethic that governs capitalist society— the idea that I will only be of service to you if it is profitable for me to be so—was a detestable way to live. We would not treat our friends or children in this way, so why should we accept it as a perfectly natural way of dealing with others in the public realm?

It is true that Marx quite often denounces morality. By this, however, he meant the kind of historical inquiry which ignores material factors in favour of moral ones. The proper term for this is not morality but moralism. Moralism abstracts something called "moral values" from the whole historical context in which they are set, and then generally proceeds to hand down absolute moral judgements. A truly moral inquiry, by contrast, is one which investigates all the aspects of a human situation. It refuses to divorce human values, behavior, relationships and qualities of character from the social and historical forces which shape them. It thus escapes the false distinction between moral judgement on the one hand and scientific analysis on the other. A true moral judgement needs to examine all the relevant facts as rigorously as possible. In this sense, Marx himself was a true moralist in the tradition of Aristotle, though he did not always know that he was.

Moreover, he belonged to the great Aristotelian tradition for which morality was not primarily a question of laws, obligations, codes and prohibitions, but a question of how to live in the freest, fullest, most self-fulfilling way. Morality for Marx was in the end all about enjoying yourself. But since nobody can live their lives in isolation, ethics had to involve politics as well. Aristotle thought just the same.

The spiritual is indeed about the otherworldly. But it is not the otherworldly as the parsons conceive of it. It is the other world which socialists hope to build in the future, in place of one which is clearly past its sell-by date. Anyone who isn't otherworldly in this sense has obviously not taken a good hard look around them.

SEVEN

Nothing is more outdated about Marxism than its tedious obsession with class. Marxists seem not to have noticed that the landscape of social class has changed almost out of recognition since the days when Marx himself was writing. In particular, the working class which they fondly imagine will usher in socialism has disappeared almost without trace. We live in a social world where class matters less and less, where there is more and more social mobility, and where talk of class struggle is as archaic as talk of burning heretics at the stake. The revolutionary worker, like the wicked top-hatted capitalist, is a figment of the Marxist imagination.

We have seen already that Marxists have a problem with the idea of utopia. This is one reason why they reject the illusion that, just because chief executives nowadays might sport sneakers, listen to Rage Against the Machine and beseech their employees to call them "Cuddlykins," social class has been swept from the face of the earth. Marxism does not define class in terms of style, status, income, accent, occupation or whether you have ducks or Degas on the wall. Socialist men and women have not fought and sometimes died over the centuries simply to bring an end to snobbery.

The quaint American concept of "classism" would seem to suggest that class is mostly a question of attitude. The middle class should stop feeling contemptuous of the working class rather as whites should stop feeling superior to African-Americans. But Marxism is not a question of attitude. Class for Marxism, rather like virtue for Aristotle, is not a matter of how you are feeling but of what you are doing. It is a question of where you stand within a particular mode of production—whether as slave, self-employed peasant, agricultural tenant, owner of capital, financier, seller of one's labour power, petty proprietor and so on. Marxism has not been put out of business because Etonians have started to drop their aitches, princes of the royal household puke in the gutter outside nightclubs, or some more antique forms of class distinction have been blurred by the universal solvent known as money. The fact that the European aristocracy are honoured to hobnob with Mick Jagger has signally failed to usher in the classless society.

We have heard a good deal about the supposed disappearance of the working class. Before we turn to that topic, however, what of the less-heralded passing of the traditional haute bourgeoisie or upper-middle class? As Perry Anderson has noted, the kind of men and women unforgettably portrayed by novelists such as Marcel Proust and Thomas Mann are now all but extinct. "By and large," Anderson writes, "the bourgeoisie as Baudelaire or Marx, Ibsen or Rimbaud, Groz or Brecht—or even Sartre or O'Hara—knew it, is a thing of the past." Socialists, however, should not get too excited by this obituary notice. For as Anderson goes on to remark, "In place of that solid amphitheatre is an aquarium of floating, evanescent forms—the projectors and managers, auditors and janitors, administrators and speculators of contemporary capital: functions of a monetary universe that knows no social fixities or stable identities."[1] Class changes its composition all the time. But this does not mean that it vanishes without trace.

It is in the nature of capitalism to confound distinctions, collapse hierarchies and mix the most diverse forms of life promiscuously together. No form of life is more hybrid and pluralistic. When it comes to who exactly should be exploited, the system is admirably egalitarian. It is as antihierarchical as the most pious postmodernist, and as generously inclusivist as the most earnest Anglican vicar. It is anxious to leave absolutely nobody out. Where there is profit to be made, black and white, women and men, toddlers and senior citizens, neighbourhoods in Wakefield and rural villages in Sumatra are all grist to its mill, to be treated with impeccable evenhandedness. It is the commodity form, not socialism, that is the great leveller. The commodity does not check up on where its potential consumer went to school, or whether she pronounces "basin" to rhyme with "bison." It imposes just the kind of uniformity that, as we have seen, Marx sets his face against.

We should not be surprised, then, that advanced capitalism breeds delusions of classlessness. This is not just a façade behind which the system conceals its true inequities; it is in the nature of the beast. Even so, there is a telling contrast between the dressed-down matiness of the modern office and a global system in which distinctions of wealth and power yawn wider than ever. Old-style hierarchies may have yielded in some sectors of the economy to decentralised, network-based, team-oriented, information-rich, first-name, open-neck-shirted forms of organisation. But capital remains concentrated in fewer hands than ever before, and the ranks of the destitute and dispossessed swell by the hour. While the chief executive smoothes his jeans over his sneakers, over one billion on the planet go hungry every day. Most of the megacities in the south of the globe are stinking slums rife with disease and overcrowding, and slum dwellers represent one-third of the global urban population. The urban poor more generally constitute at least one-half of the world's population.[2] Meanwhile, some in the West seek in their evangelical fervor to spread liberal democracy to the rest of the globe, at the very point that the world's destiny is being determined by a handful of Western-based corporations answerable to nobody but their shareholders.

Even so, Marxists are not simply "against" the capitalist class, as one might be against hunting or smoking. We have seen already that no one admired their magnificent achievements more than Marx himself. It was on these achievements—a resolute opposition to political tyranny, a massive accumulation of wealth which brought with it the prospect of universal prosperity, respect for the individual, civil liberties, democratic rights, a truly international community and so on—that socialism itself would need to build. Class-history was to be used, not simply discarded. Capitalism, as we have noted, had proved an emancipatory force as well as a catastrophic one; and it is Marxism, more than any other political theory, which seeks to deliver a judicious account of it, in contrast with mindless celebration on the one hand and blanket condemnation on the other. Among the mighty gifts that capitalism bestowed on the world, however unintentionally, was the working class—a social force which it reared up for its own self-interested purposes to the point where it became in principle capable of taking it over. This is one reason why irony lies at the heart of Marx's vision of history. There is a dark humour in the vision of the capitalist order giving birth to its own gravedigger.

Marxism does not focus on the working class because it sees some resplendent virtue in labour. Burglars and bankers toil away too, but Marx was not notable for his championship of them. (He did, however, once write about housebreaking, in a splendid parody of his own economic theory.) Marxism, as we have seen, wants to abolish labour as far as possible. Nor does it assign such political importance to the working class because it is supposedly the most downtrodden of social groups. There are many such groups—vagrants, students, refugees, the elderly, the unemployed and chronically unemployable—who are often more needy than the average worker. The working class does not cease to interest Marxists the moment it acquires indoor bathrooms or colour television. It is its place within the capitalist mode of production which is most decisive. Only those within that system, familiar with its workings, organised by it into a skilled, politically conscious collective force, indispensable to its successful running yet with a material interest in bringing it low, can feasibly take it over and run it instead for the benefit of all. No well-meaning paternalist or bunch of outside agitators can do it for them—which is to say that Marx's attention to the working class (by far the majority of the population of his time) is inseparable from his deep respect for democracy.

If Marx assigns the working class such importance, it is among other things because he sees them as the bearers of a universal emancipation:

> A class must be formed which has *radical chains,* a class in civil society which is not a class of civil society, a class which is the dissolution of all classes, a sphere of society which has a universal character because its sufferings are universal, and which does not claim a *particular redress* because the wrong which is done to it is not a *particular wrong* but

> *wrong in general.* There must be formed a sphere of
> society which claims no *traditional* status but only a
> human status . . . which is, in short, a *total loss* of
> humanity and which can only redeem itself by a
> *total redemption of humanity.* This dissolution of
> society, as a particular class, is the *proletariat* . . .[3]

The working class for Marx is in one sense a specific social group. Yet because it signifies for him the wrong which keeps so many other kinds of wrong in business (imperial wars, colonial expansion, famine, genocide, the plundering of Nature, to some extent racism and patriarchy), it has a significance far beyond its own sphere. In this sense, it resembles the scapegoat in ancient societies, which is cast out of the city because it represents a universal crime, but which for just the same reason has the power to become the cornerstone of a new social order. Because it is both necessary to and excluded by the capitalist system, this "class which is not a class" is a kind of riddle or conundrum. In a quite literal sense, it creates the social order—it is on its silent, persistent labour that the whole mighty edifice is reared—yet it can find no real representation within that order, no full recognition of its humanity. It is both functional and dispossessed, specific and universal, an integral part of civil society yet a kind of nothing.

Because the very foundation of society is in this sense self-contradictory, the working class signifies the point at which the whole logic of that order begins to unravel and dissolve. It is the joker in the pack of civilisation, the factor which is neither securely inside nor outside it, the place where that form of life is forced to confront the very contradictions that constitute it. Because the working class has no real stake in the status quo, it is partly invisible within it; but for just the same reason it can prefigure an alternative future. It is the "dissolution" of society in the sense of its negation—the garbage or waste product for which the social order can find no real place. In this sense, it acts as a sign of just what a radical breaking and remaking would be needed to include it. But it is also the dissolution of present society in a more positive sense, as the class which when it comes to power will finally abolish class-society altogether. Individuals will then finally be free of the straitjacket of social class, and will be able to flourish as themselves. In this sense, the working class is also "universal" because in seeking to transform its own condition, it can also ring down the curtain on the whole squalid narrative of class-society as such.

Here, then, is another irony or contradiction—the fact that it is only through class that class can be overcome. If Marxism is so taken with the concept of class, it is only because it wants to see the back of it. Marx himself seems to have viewed social class as a form of alienation. To call men and women simply "workers" or "capitalists" is to bury their unique individuality beneath a faceless category. But it is an alienation that can be undone only from the inside. Only by going all the way through class, accepting it as an unavoidable social reality rather than wishing it piously away, can it be dismantled. It is just the same with race and gender. It is not enough to treat every individual as unique, as with those American liberals for whom everyone (including, presumably, Donald Trump and the Boston Strangler) is "special." The fact that people are massed anonymously together may be in one sense an alienation, but in another sense it is a condition of their emancipation. Once again, history moves by its "bad" side. Well-meaning liberals who regard every member of the Ruritanian Liberation Movement as a unique individual have failed to grasp the purpose of the Ruritanian Liberation Movement. Its aim is to get to the point where Ruritanians can indeed be free to be themselves. If they could be that right now, however, they would not need their Liberation Movement.

There is another sense in which Marxism looks beyond the working class in the act of looking to it. No self-respecting socialist has ever believed that the working class can bring down capitalism all by itself. Only by forging political alliances is such a daunting task conceivable. Marx himself thought that the working class should support the petty bourgeois peasantry, not least in countries like France, Russia and Germany where industrial workers were still a minority. The Bolsheviks sought to forge a united front of workers, poor peasants, soldiers, sailors, urban intellectuals and so on.

It is worth noting in this respect that the original proletariat was not the blue-collar male working class. It was lower-class women in ancient society. The word "proletariat" comes to us from the Latin word for "offspring," meaning those who were too poor to serve the state with anything but their wombs. Too deprived to contribute to economic life in any other way, these women produced labour power in the form of children. They had nothing to yield up but the fruit of their bodies. What society demanded from them was not production but reproduction. The proletariat started life among those outside the labour process, not those within it. Yet the labour they endured was a lot more painful than breaking boulders.

Today, in an era of Third World sweatshops and agricultural labour, the typical proletarian is still a woman. White-collar work which in Victorian times was performed mostly by lower-middle-class men is nowadays largely the reserve of working-class women, who are typically paid less than unskilled male manual workers. It was women, too, who mostly staffed the huge expansion in shop and clerical work which followed the decline in heavy industry after the First World War. In Marx's own time, the largest group of wage labourers was not the industrial working class but domestic servants, most of whom were female.

The working class, then, is not always male, brawny and handy with a sledgehammer. If you think of it that way, you will be bemused by the geographer David Harvey's claim that "the global proletariat is far larger than ever."[4] If the working class means blue-collar factory workers, then it has indeed diminished sharply in advanced capitalist societies—though this is partly because a fair slice of such work has been exported to more poverty-stricken regions of the planet. It remains true, however, that industrial employment on a global scale has declined. Yet even when Britain was the workshop of the world, manufacturing workers were outnumbered by domestic servants and agricultural labourers.[5] And the tendency for manual labour to decline and white-collar work to expand is no "postmodern" phenomenon. On the contrary, it can be dated back to the start of the twentieth century.

Marx himself did not consider that you had to engage in manual labour to count as working class. In *Capital,* for example, he ranks commercial workers on the same level as industrial ones, and refuses to identify the proletariat solely with so-called productive workers, in the sense of those who directly turn out commodities. Rather, the working class includes all those who are forced to sell their labour power to capital, who languish under its oppressive disciplines and who have little or no control over their conditions of labour. Negatively speaking, we might describe them as those who would benefit most from the fall of capitalism. In this sense, lower-level white-collar workers, who are often unskilled, with poor wages, job insecurity and little say in the labour process are to be counted among its ranks. There is a white-collar working class as well as an industrial one, which includes a great many technical, clerical and administrative workers bereft of any autonomy or authority. Class, we should recall, is a matter not just of abstract legal ownership, but the capacity to deploy one's power over others to one's own advantage.

Among those eager to preside over the funeral rites of the working class, much has been made of the immense growth in the service, information and communications sectors. The transition from industrial to "late," "consumerist," "postindustrial" or "postmodern" capitalism has indeed involved some notable changes, as we have seen earlier. But we have also seen that none of this has altered the fundamental nature of capitalist property relations. On the contrary, such changes have mostly been in the interest of expanding and consolidating them. It is also worth recalling that work in the service sector can be just as heavy, dirty and disagreeable as traditional industrial labour. We need to think not just of upmarket chefs and Harley Street receptionists but of dockers, transport, refuse, postal, hospital, cleaning and catering workers. Indeed, the distinction between manufacture and service workers, as far as pay, control and conditions go, is often well-nigh invisible. Those who work in call centres are just as exploited as those who toil in coal mines. Labels such as "service" or "white-collar" serve to obscure massive differences between, say, airline pilots and hospital porters, or senior civil servants and hotel chambermaids. As Jules Townshend comments, "To categorise lower-level white collar workers, who have no control over their labour and experience job insecurity and poor wages, as nonmembers of the working-class is intuitively questionable."[6]

In any case, the service industry itself involves a sizeable amount of manufacture. If the industrial worker has given way to the bank clerk and the barmaid, where did all the counters, desks, bars, computers and cash machines come from? A waitress, chauffeur, teaching assistant or computer operator does not count as middle class simply because he or she churns out no tangible product. As far as their material interests go, they have as much a stake in creating a more equitable social order as the most sorely exploited of wage slaves. We should keep in mind, too, the vast army of the retired, unemployed and chronically sick, who along with casual labourers are not a permanent part of the "official" labour process but who certainly count as working class.

It is true that there has been an immense expansion in technical, administrative and managerial jobs, as capitalism deploys its technology to squeeze a larger amount of goods out of a much smaller body of workers. Yet if this is no disproval of Marxism, it is partly because Marx himself took scrupulous note of it. As long ago as the mid-nineteenth century, he is to be found writing of the "constantly growing number of the middle classes," which he rebukes orthodox political economy for overlooking. These are men and women "situated midway between the workers on the one side and the capitalists on the other"[7]—a phrase that should be enough to discredit the myth that Marx reduces the complexity of modern society to two starkly polarized classes. In fact, one commentator argues that he envisaged the virtual disappearance of the proletariat as it was known in his own time. Capitalism, far from being overturned by the famished and dispossessed, would be brought low by the application of advanced scientific techniques to the production process, a situation that would produce a society of free and equal individuals. Whatever one thinks of this reading of Marx, there is no doubt that he was well aware of how the capitalist process of production was already drawing more and more technical and scientific labour into its orbit. He speaks in the *Grundrisse* of "general social knowledge [becoming] a direct productive force," a phrase that prefigures what some would now call the information society.

Yet the spread of the technical and administrative sectors has been accompanied by a progressive blurring of lines between working class and middle class. The new information technologies have spelled the disappearance of many traditional occupations, along with a drastic dwindling of economic stability, settled career structures and the idea of a vocation. One effect of this has been an increasing proletarianisation of professionals, along with a re-proletarianisation of branches of the industrial working class. As John Gray puts it, "The middle classes are rediscovering the condition of assetless economic insecurity that afflicted the nineteenth-century proletariat."[8] Many of those who would be traditionally labelled lower-middle class—teachers, social workers, technicians, journalists, middling clerical and administrative officials—have been subject to a relentless process of proletarianisation, as they come under pressure from tightening management disciplines. And this means that they are more likely to be drawn to the cause of the working class proper in the event of a political crisis.

It would, of course, be an excellent thing for socialists if top managers, administrators and business executives were to throw in their hand with their cause as well. Marxists have nothing against judges, rock stars, media magnates and major-generals flooding enthusiastically into their ranks. There is no ban on Rupert Murdoch and Paris Hilton, as long as they were to prove suitably repentant and undergo a lengthy period of penance. Even Martin Amis and Tom Cruise might be granted some form of junior, strictly temporary membership. It is just that such individuals, given their social status and material position, are more likely to identify with the current system. If, however, it was for some curious reason in the interests of fashion designers but not postal workers to see an end to that system, then Marxists would focus their political attention on fashion designers and strongly oppose the advance of postal workers.

The situation, then, is by no means as clear-cut as the Death-of-the-Worker ideologues would suggest. In the top echelons of society we have what can justly be called the ruling class, though it is by no means a conspiracy of wicked capitalists. Its ranks include aristocrats, judges, senior lawyers and clerics, media barons, top military brass and media commentators, high-ranking politicians, police officers and civil servants, professors (a few of them political renegades), big landlords, bankers, stockbrokers, industrialists, chief executives, heads of public schools and so on. Most of these are not capitalists themselves, but act, however indirectly, as the agents of capital. Whether they live off capital, rents or salaried incomes makes no difference to this point. Not all those who earn a wage or salary are working class. Think of Britney Spears. Below this top social layer stretches a stratum of middle-class managers, scientists, administrators, bureaucrats and the like; and below them in turn lies a range of lower-middle-class occupations such as teachers, social workers and junior managers. The working class proper can then be taken to encompass both manual labourers and the lower levels of white-collar workers: clerical, technical, administrative, service and so on. And this is a massive proportion of the world population. Chris Harman estimates the size of the global working class at around two billion, with a similar number being subject to much the same economic logic.[9] Another estimate puts it at around three billion.[10] The working class seems to have disappeared rather less successfully than Lord Lucan.[11]

Nor should one forget the enormous slum population of the world, growing at an extraordinarily fast rate. If slum dwellers do not already form a majority of the global urban population, they soon will. These men and women are not part of the working class in the classical sense of the term, but neither do they fall entirely outside the productive process. They tend rather to drift in and out of it, working typically in low-paid, unskilled, unprotected casual services without contracts, rights, regulations or bargaining power. They include hawkers, hustlers, garment workers, food and drink sellers, prostitutes, child labourers, rickshaw pullers, domestic servants and small-time self-employed entrepreneurs. Marx himself distinguishes between different layers of the unemployed; and what he has to say about the "floating" unemployed or casual labourer of his own day, who count for him as part of the working class, sounds very similar to the condition of many of today's slum dwellers. If they are not routinely exploited, they are certainly economically oppressed; and taken together they form the fastest growing social group on earth. If they can be easy fodder for right-wing religious movements, they can also muster some impressive acts of political resistance. In Latin America, this informal economy now employs over half the workforce. They form an informal proletariat which has shown itself well capable of political organisation; and if they were to revolt against their dire conditions, there is no doubt the world capitalist system would be shaken to its roots.

Marx held that the concentration of working people in factories was a precondition of their political emancipation. By bringing workers physically together for its own self-interested purposes, capitalism created the conditions in which they could organise themselves politically, which was not quite what the system's rulers had in mind. Capitalism cannot survive without a working class, while the working class can flourish a lot more freely without capitalism. Those who dwell in the slums of the world's megacities are not organised at the point of production, but there is no reason to suppose that this is the only place where the wretched of the earth can conspire to transform their situation. Like the classical proletariat, they exist as a collective, have the strongest possible interest in the passing of the present world order, and have nothing to lose but their chains.[12]

The demise of the working class, then, has been much exaggerated. There are those who speak of a shift in radical circles away from class to race, gender and postcolonialism. We shall be examining this a little later. In the meantime, we should note that only those for whom class is a matter of frock-coated factory owners and boiler-suited workers could embrace such a simpleminded notion. Convinced that class is as dead as the Cold War, they turn instead to culture, identity, ethnicity and sexuality. In today's world, however, these things are as interwoven with social class as they ever were.

EIGHT

Marxists are advocates of violent political action. They reject a sensible course of moderate, piecemeal reform and opt instead for the bloodstained chaos of revolution. A small band of insurrectionists will rise up, overthrow the state and impose its will on the majority. This is one of several senses in which Marxism and democracy are at daggers drawn. Because they despise morality as mere ideology, Marxists are not especially troubled by the mayhem their politics would unleash on the population. The end justifies the means, however many lives may be lost in the process.

The idea of revolution usually evokes images of violence and chaos. In this, it can be contrasted with social reform, which we tend to think of as peaceful, moderate and gradual. This, however, is a false opposition. Many reforms have been anything but peaceful. Think of the United States civil rights movement, which was far from revolutionary yet which involved death, beatings, lynchings and brutal repression. In the colonial-dominated Latin America of the eighteenth and nineteenth centuries, every attempt at liberal reform sparked off violent social conflict.

Some revolutions, by contrast, have been relatively peaceful. There are velvet revolutions as well as violent ones. Not many people died in the Dublin uprising of 1916, which was to result in partial independence for Ireland. Surprisingly little blood was spilt in the Bolshevik revolution of 1917. In fact, the actual takeover of key points in Moscow was accomplished without a shot being fired. The government, in the words of Isaac Deutscher, "was elbowed out of existence by a slight push,"[1] so overwhelming was the support of the common people for the insurgents. When the Soviet system fell over seventy years later, this sprawling landmass with a ferocious history of conflict collapsed without much more bloodshed than had occurred on the day of its foundation.

It is true that a bloody civil war followed hard on the heels of the Bolshevik revolution. But this was because the new social order came under savage attack from right-wing forces as well as foreign invaders. British and French forces backed the counterrevolutionary White forces to the hilt.

For Marxism, a revolution is not characterized by how much violence it involves. Nor is it a total upheaval. Russia did not wake up on the morning after the Bolshevik revolution to find all market relations abolished and all industry publicly owned. On the contrary, markets and private property survived for a considerable time after the Bolshevik seizure of power, and for the most part the Bolsheviks approached their dismantling in gradualist spirit. The left wing of the party took a similar line with the peasantry. There was no question of driving them into collective farms by force; instead, the process was to be gradual and consensual.

Revolutions are usually a long time in the brewing, and may take centuries to achieve their goals. The middle classes of Europe did not abolish feudalism overnight. Seizing political power is a short-term affair; transforming the customs, institutions and habits of feeling of a society takes a great deal longer. You can socialise industry by government decree, but legislation alone cannot produce men and women who feel and behave differently from their grandparents. That involves a lengthy process of education and cultural change.

Those who doubt that such change is possible should take a long hard look at themselves. For we in modern Britain are ourselves the products of a long revolution, one which came to a head in the seventeenth century; and the chief sign of its success is that most of us are completely unaware of the fact. Successful revolutions are those which end up by erasing all traces of themselves. In doing so, they make the situation they struggled to bring about seem entirely natural. In this, they are a bit like childbirth. To operate as "normal" human beings, we have to forget the anguish and terror of our births. Origins are usually traumatic, whether of individuals or political states. Marx reminds us in *Capital* that the modern British state, built on the intensive exploitation of peasants-turned-proletarians, came into existence dripping blood and dirt from every pore. This is one reason why he would have been horrified to observe Stalin's forced urbanization of the Russian peasantry. Most political states came about through revolution, invasion, occupation, usurpation or (in the case of societies like the United States) extermination. Successful states are those that have managed to wipe this bloody history from the minds of their citizens. States whose unjust origins are too recent for this to be possible—Israel and Northern Ireland, for example—are likely to be plagued with political conflict.

If we ourselves are the products of a supremely successful revolution, then this in itself is an answer to the conservative charge that all revolutions end up by failing, or reverting to how things were before, or making things a thousand times worse, or eating up their own children. Perhaps I missed the announcement in the newspapers, but France does not seem to have reinstated the feudal aristocracy in government, or Germany the landowning Junkers. Britain, it is true, has more feudal remnants than most modern nations, from the House of Lords to Black Rod, but this is largely because they prove useful to the ruling middle classes. Like the monarchy, they generate the kind of mystique that is supposed to keep the mass of the people suitably daunted and deferential. That most British people do not see Prince Andrew as exuding a seductive air of mystery and enigma suggests that there may be more reliable ways of propping up your power.

Most people in the West at present would no doubt declare themselves opposed to revolution. What this probably means is that they are against some revolutions and in favour of others. Other people's revolutions, like other people's food in restaurants, are usually more attractive than one's own. Most of these people would doubtless approve of the revolution that unseated British power in America at the end of the eighteenth century, or the fact that colonized nations from Ireland and India to Kenya and Malaysia finally won their independence. It is unlikely that many of them wept bitter tears over the fall of the Soviet bloc. Slave uprisings from Spartacus to the southern states of America are likely to meet with their approval. Yet all these insurrections involved violence—in some cases, more violence than the Bolshevik revolution did. So would it not be more honest to come clean and confess that it is socialist revolution one objects to, not revolution itself?

There is, of course, a small minority of people known as pacifists who reject violence altogether. Their courage and firmness of principle, often in the teeth of public revilement, are much to be admired. But pacifists are not just people who abhor violence. Almost everyone does that, with the exception of a thin sprinkling of sadists and psychopaths. For pacifism to be worth arguing with, it must be more than some pious declaration that war is disgusting. Cases with which almost everyone would agree are boring, however sound they may be. The only pacifist worth arguing with is one who rejects violence absolutely. And that means rejecting not just wars or revolutions, but refusing to tap an escaped murderer smartly over the skull, enough to stun but not kill him, when he is about to turn his machine gun on a classroom of small children. Anyone who was in a situation to do this and failed to do so would have a lot of explaining to do at the next meeting of the PTA. In any strict sense of the word, pacifism is grossly immoral. Almost everyone agrees with the need to use violence in extreme and exceptional circumstances. The United Nations Charter permits armed resistance to an occupying power. It is just that any such aggression has to be hedged round with some severe qualifications. It must be primarily defensive, it must be the last resort after all else has been tried and failed, it must be the only means to undo some major evil, it must be proportionate, it must have a reasonable chance of success, it should not involve the slaughter of innocent civilians and so on.

In its brief but bloody career, Marxism has involved a hideous amount of violence. Both Stalin and Mao Zedong were mass murderers on an almost unimaginable scale. Yet very few Marxists today, as we have seen already, would seek to defend these horrific crimes, whereas many non-Marxists would defend, say, the destruction of Dresden or Hiroshima. I have already argued that Marxists have offered far more persuasive explanations of how the atrocities of men like Stalin came about, and thus how they can be prevented from happening again, than any other school of thought. But what of the crimes of capitalism? What of the atrocious bloodbath known as the First World War, in which the clash of imperial nations hungry for territory sent working-class soldiers to a futile death? The history of capitalism is among other things a story of global warfare, colonial exploitation, genocide and avoidable famines. If a distorted version of Marxism gave birth to the Stalinist state, an extreme mutation of capitalism produced the fascist one. If a million men and women died in the Great Irish Famine of the 1840s, it was to a large extent because the British government of the day insisted on observing the laws of the free market in its lamentable relief policy. We have seen that Marx writes with scarcely suppressed outrage in *Capital* of the bloody, protracted process by which the English peasantry were driven from the land. It is this history of violent expropriation which lies beneath the tranquility of the English rural landscape. Compared to this horrendous episode, one which stretched over a lengthy period of time, an event like the Cuban revolution was a tea party.

For Marxists, antagonism is built into the very nature of capitalism. This is true not only of the class conflict it involves, but of the wars to which it gives rise, as capitalist nations clash over global resources or spheres of imperial influence. By contrast, one of the most urgent goals of the international socialist movement has been peace. When the

Bolsheviks came to power, they withdrew Russia from the carnage of the First World War. Socialists, with their hatred of militarism and chauvinism, have played a major role in most peace movements throughout modern history. The working-class movement has not been about violence, but about putting an end to it.

Marxists have also been traditionally hostile to what they call "adventurism," by which they mean recklessly throwing a small band of revolutionaries against the colossal forces of the state. The Bolshevik revolution was made not by a secret coterie of conspirators but by individuals openly elected in the popular, representative institutions known as soviets. Marx set his face resolutely against mock-heroic uprisings by grim-faced militants brandishing pitchforks against tanks. In his view, successful revolution required certain material preconditions. It is not just a question of a steely will and a hefty dose of courage. You are obviously likely to fare much better in the midst of a major crisis in which the governing class is weak and divided, and socialist forces are robust and well-organised, than when the government is buoyant and the opposition is timorous and fragmented. In this sense, there is a relation between Marx's materialism—his insistence on analyzing the material forces at work in society—and the question of revolutionary violence.

Most working-class protest in Britain, from the Chartists to the hunger marches of the 1930s, has been peaceful. On the whole, working-class movements have resorted to violence only when provoked, or at times of compelling need, or when peaceful tactics have clearly failed. Much the same was true of the Suffragettes. The reluctance of working people to shed blood has contrasted tellingly with the readiness of their masters to wield the lash and the gun. Nor have they had at their disposal anything like the formidable military resources of the capitalist state. In many parts of the world today, a repressive state, prepared to roll out its weapons against peaceable strikers and demonstrators, has become a commonplace. As the German philosopher Walter Benjamin wrote, revolution is not a runaway train; it is the application of the emergency brake. It is capitalism which is out of control, driven as it is by the anarchy of market forces, and socialism which attempts to reassert some collective mastery over this rampaging beast.

If socialist revolutions have generally involved violence, it is largely because propertied classes will rarely surrender their privileges without a struggle. Even so, there are reasonable grounds to hope that such use of force can be kept to a minimum. This is because a revolution for Marxism is not the same thing as a coup d'etat, or an outbreak of spontaneous disaffection. Revolutions are not just attempts to bring down the state. A right-wing military coup might do that, but it is not what Marxists regard as a revolution. In the fullest sense, revolutions come about only when one social class overthrows the rule of another and replaces it with its own power.

Why Marx Was Right

In the case of socialist revolution, this means that the organised working class, along with its various allies, take over from the bourgeoisie, or capitalist middle class. But Marx regarded the working class as by far the largest class in capitalist society. So we are speaking here of the actions of a majority, not of a small bunch of rebels. Since socialism is about popular self-government, nobody can make a socialist revolution on your behalf, just as nobody can become an expert poker player on your behalf. As G. K. Chesterton writes, such popular self-determination is "a thing analogous to writing one's own love letters or blowing one's own nose. These are things we want a man to do for himself, even if he does them badly."[2] My valet may be a great deal more dexterous at blowing my nose than I am myself, but it befits my dignity that I do it myself, or (if I am Prince Charles) at least every now and then. Revolution cannot be handed down to you by a tight-knit vanguard of conspirators. Nor, as Lenin insisted, can it be carried abroad and imposed at the point of a bayonet, as Stalin did in eastern Europe. You have to be actively involved in the making of it yourself, unlike the kind of artist who instructs his assistants to go off and pickle a shark in his name. (No doubt the same will soon be happening with novelists.) Only then will those who were once relatively powerless have the experience, know-how and self-assurance to go on to remake society as a whole. Socialist revolutions can only be democratic ones. It is the ruling class which is the undemocratic minority. And the large masses of people that such insurrections must involve by their very nature are their surest bulwark against excessive force. In this sense, revolutions which are likely to be successful are also likely to be the least violent.

This is not to say that revolutions may not provoke a bloody backlash from panic-stricken governments prepared to unleash terror against them. But even autocratic states have to rely on a certain amount of passive consent from those they govern, however grudging and provisional. You cannot adequately govern a nation which is not only in a permanent state of disaffection, but which denies any shred of credibility to your rule. You can imprison some of the people some of the time, but not all of the people all of the time. It is possible for such discredited states to hang on for quite long periods. Think, for example, of the current regimes in Burma or Zimbabwe. In the end, however, it can become clear even to tyrants that the writing is on the wall. However cruel and murderous the apartheid system of South Africa was, it eventually came to recognize that it could no longer carry on. The same can be said of the dictatorships of Poland, East Germany, Romania and other Soviet-controlled nations at the end of the 1980s. It is also true of many Ulster Unionists today, who after years of bloodshed have been forced to recognize that their exclusion of Catholic citizens is simply no longer viable.

Why, though, do Marxists look to revolution rather than to parliamentary democracy and social reform? The answer is that they do not, or at least not entirely. Only so-called ultra-leftists do this.[3] One of the first decrees of the Bolsheviks when they came to power in Russia was to abolish the death penalty. Being a reformist or a revolutionary is not like supporting either Everton or Arsenal. Most revolutionaries are also champions of reform. Not any old reform, and not reformism as a political panacea; but revolutionaries expect socialist change to come all in a rush no more than feudal or capitalist change did. Where they differ from reformists proper is not, say, in refusing to fight against hospital closures because they distract attention from the all-important Revolution. It is rather that they view such reforms in a longer, more radical perspective. Reform is vital; but sooner or later you will hit a point where the system refuses to give way, and for Marxism this is known as the social relations of production. Or, in less politely technical language, a dominant class which controls the material resources and is markedly reluctant to hand them over. It is only then that a decisive choice between reform and revolution looms up. In the end, as the socialist historian R. H. Tawney remarked, you can peel an onion layer by layer, but you can't skin a tiger claw by claw. Peeling an onion, however, makes reform sound rather too easy. Most of the reforms we now regard as precious features of liberal society—universal suffrage, free universal education, freedom of the press, trade unions and so on—were won by popular struggle in the teeth of ferocious ruling-class resistance.

Nor do revolutionaries necessarily reject parliamentary democracy. If it can contribute to their goals, so much the better. Marxists, however, have reservations about parliamentary democracy—not because it is democratic, but because it is not democratic enough. Parliaments are institutions to which ordinary people are persuaded to permanently delegate their power, and over which they have very little control. Revolution is generally thought to be the opposite of democracy, as the work of sinister underground minorities out to subvert the will of the majority. In fact, as a process by which men and women assume power over their own existence through popular councils and assemblies, it is a great deal more democratic than anything on offer at the moment. The Bolsheviks had an impressive record of open controversy within their ranks, and the idea that they should rule the country as the only political party was no part of their original programme. Besides, as we shall see later, parliaments are part of a state which is in business, by and large, to ensure the sovereignty of capital over labour. This is not just the opinion of Marxists. As one seventeenth-century commentator wrote, the English parliament is the "bulwark of property."[4] In the end, so Marx claims, parliament or the state represents not so much the common people as the interests of private property. Cicero, as we have seen, heartily agreed. No parliament in a capitalist order would dare to confront the awesome power of such vested interests. If it threatened to interfere with them too radically, it would quickly be shown the door. It would be odd, then, for socialists to regard such debating chambers as a vital means of promoting their cause, rather than as one means among many.

Marx himself seems to have believed that in countries like England, Holland and the United States, socialists might achieve their goals by peaceful means. He did not dismiss parliament or social reform. He also thought that a socialist party could assume power only with the support of a majority of the working class. He was an enthusiastic champion of reformist organs such as working-class political parties, trade unions, cultural associations and political newspapers. He also spoke out for specific reformist measures such as the extension of the franchise and the shortening of the working day. In fact at one point he considered rather optimistically that universal suffrage would itself undermine capitalist rule. His collaborator Friedrich Engels also attached a good deal of importance to peaceful social change, and looked forward to a nonviolent revolution.

One of the problems with socialist revolutions is that they are most likely to break out in places where they are hardest to sustain. Lenin noted this irony in the case of the Bolshevik uprising. Men and women who are cruelly oppressed and semistarving may feel they have nothing to lose in making a revolution. On the other hand, as we have seen, the backward social conditions which drive them to revolt are the worst possible place to begin to build socialism. It may be easier in these conditions to overthrow the state, but you do not have to hand the resources that would allow you to build a viable alternative. People who feel content with their condition are not likely to launch revolutions. But neither are people who feel bereft of hope. The bad news for socialists is that men and women will be extremely reluctant to transform their situation as long as there is still something in that situation for them.

Marxists are sometimes taunted with the supposed political apathy of the working class. Ordinary people may well be indifferent to the day-to-day politics of a state which they feel is indifferent to them. Once it tries to close their hospitals, shift their factory to the west of Ireland or plant an airport in their back gardens, however, they are likely to be stirred into action. It is also worth emphasizing that apathy of a kind may be entirely rational. As long as a social system can still yield its citizens some meagre gratification, it is not unreasonable for them to stick with what they have, rather than take a perilous leap into an unknowable future. Conservatism of this kind is not to be scoffed at.

Why Marx Was Right

In any case, most people are too preoccupied with keeping themselves afloat to bother with visions of the future. Social disruption, understandably enough, is not something most men and women are eager to embrace. They will certainly not embrace it just because socialism sounds like a good idea. It is when the deprivations of the status quo begin to outweigh the drawbacks of radical change that a leap into the future begins to seem a reasonable proposition. Revolutions tend to break out when almost any alternative seems preferable to the present. In that situation, not to rebel would be irrational. Capitalism cannot complain when, having appealed for centuries to the supremacy of self-interest, its hirelings recognize that their collective self-interest lies in trying something different for a change.

Reform and social democracy can certainly buy off revolution. Marx himself lived long enough to witness the beginnings of this process in Victorian Britain, but not long enough to register its full impact. If a class-society can throw its minions enough scraps and leavings, it is probably safe for the time being. Once it fails to do so, it is very likely (though by no means inevitable) that those on the losing end will seek to take it over. Why should they not? How could anything be worse than no scraps or leavings at all? At this point, placing your bets on an alternative future becomes an eminently rational decision. And though reason in human beings does not go all the way down, it is robust enough to know when abandoning the present for the future is almost certain to be to its advantage.

Those who ask who is going to bring capitalism low tend to forget that in one sense this is unnecessary. Capitalism is perfectly capable of collapsing under its own contradictions without even the slightest shove from its opponents. In fact, it came fairly near to doing so just a few years ago. The result of a wholesale implosion of the system, however, is more likely to be barbarism than socialism, if there is no organised political force at hand to offer an alternative. One urgent reason why we need such organisation, then, is that in the event of an almighty crisis of capitalism, fewer people are likely to get hurt, and a new system of benefit to all may be plucked from the ruins.

NINE

Marxism believes in an all-powerful state. Having abol-
ished private property, socialist revolutionaries will rule by
means of a despotic power, and that power will put an end to
individual freedom. This has happened wherever Marxism
has been put into practice; there is no reason to expect that
things would be different in the future. It is part of the logic
of Marxism that the people give way to the party, the party
gives way to the state, and the state to a monstrous dictator.
Liberal democracy may not be perfect, but it is infinitely
preferable to being locked in a psychiatric hospital for dar-
ing to criticize a savagely authoritarian government.

Marx was an implacable opponent of the state. In fact, he
famously looked forward to a time when it would wither
away. His critics might find this hope absurdly utopian, but
they cannot convict him at the same time of a zeal for despotic
government.

He was not, as it happens, being absurdly utopian.
What Marx hoped would wither away in communist society
was not the state in the sense of a central administration. Any
complex modern culture would require this. In fact, Marx
writes in the third volume of *Capital,* with this point in mind,

of "common activities arising from the nature of all communities." The state as an administrative body would live on. It is the state as an instrument of violence that Marx hopes to see the back of. As he puts it in the *Communist Manifesto,* public power under communism would lose its political character. Against the anarchists of his day, Marx insists that only in this sense would the state vanish from view. What had to go was a particular kind of power, one that underpinned the rule of a dominant social class over the rest of society. National parks and driving test centres would remain.

Marx views the state with cold-eyed realism. It was obviously not a politically neutral organ, scrupulously even-handed in its treatment of clashing social interests. It was not in the least dispassionate in the conflict between labour and capital. States are not in the business of launching revolutions against property. They exist among other things to defend the current social order against those who seek to transform it. If that order is inherently unjust, then in this respect the state is unjust as well. It is this that Marx wants to see an end to, not national theatres or police laboratories.

There is nothing darkly conspiratorial about the idea that the state is partisan. Anyone who thinks so has clearly not taken part in a political demonstration recently. The liberal state is neutral between capitalism and its critics until the critics look like they're winning. Then it moves in with its water hoses and paramilitary squads, and if these fail with its tanks. Nobody doubts that the state can be violent. It is just that Marx gives a new kind of answer to the question of who this violence ultimately serves. It is belief in the state's disinterestedness which is starry-eyed, not the proposal that we might one day get along without its knee-jerk aggression. In fact, even the state has ceased in some ways to believe in its own disinterestedness. Police who beat up striking workers or peaceful demonstrators no longer even pretend to be neutral. Governments, not least Labour ones, do not bother to conceal their hostility to the labour movement. As Jacques Rancière comments, "Marx's once scandalous thesis that governments are simple business agents for international capital is today an obvious fact on which 'liberals' and 'socialists' agree. The absolute identification of politics with the management of capital is no longer the shameful secret hidden behind the 'forms' of democracy; it is the openly declared truth by which our governments acquire legitimacy."[1]

This is not to suggest that we can dispense with police, law courts, prisons or even paramilitary squads. The latter, for example, might prove necessary if a gang of terrorists armed with chemical or nuclear weapons was on the loose, and the more tender-minded species of left-winger had better acknowledge the fact. Not all state violence is in the name of protecting the status quo. Marx himself draws a distinction in volume three of *Capital* between the class-specific and class-neutral functions of the state. Police officers who prevent racist thugs from beating a young Asian to death are not acting as agents of capitalism. Dedicated suites for women who have been raped are not sinister examples of state repression. Detectives who cart off computers loaded with child pornography are not brutally violating human rights. As long as there is human freedom there will also be abuses of it; and some of these abuses will be horrendous enough for the perpetrators to need locking away for the safety of others. Prisons are not just places for penalizing the socially deprived, though they are certainly that as well.

There is no evidence that Marx would have rejected any of these claims. In fact, he believed that the state could be a powerful force for good. This is why he vigorously supported legislation to improve social conditions in Victorian England. There is nothing repressive about running orphanages for abandoned children, or ensuring that everyone drives on the same side of the road. What Marx rejected was the sentimental myth of the state as a source of harmony, peacefully uniting different groups and classes. In his view, it was more a source of division than of concord. It did indeed seek to hold society together, but it did so ultimately in the interests of the governing class. Beneath its apparent evenhandedness lay a robust partisanship. The institution of the state "bound new fetters on the poor, and gave new powers to the rich ... fixed forever the laws of property and inequality; converted clever usurpation into inalienable right; and for the sake of a few ambitious men, subjected all mankind to perpetual labour, servitude and misery." These are not Marx's words, but (as we have seen already) those of Jean-Jacques Rousseau in his *Discourse on Inequality*. Marx was no lone eccentric in seeing a relation between state power and class privilege. It is true that he did not always hold these views. As a young disciple of Hegel, he spoke of the state in glowingly positive terms. But this was before he became a Marxist. And even when he became a Marxist, he insisted that he wasn't one.

Those who speak of harmony and consensus should beware of what one might call the industrial chaplain view of reality. The idea, roughly speaking, is that there are greedy bosses on one side and belligerent workers on the other, while in the middle, as the very incarnation of reason, equity and moderation, stands the decent, soft-spoken, liberal-minded chaplain who tries selflessly to bring the two warring parties together. But why should the middle always be the most sensible place to stand? Why do we tend to see ourselves as in the middle and other people as on the extremes? After all, one person's moderation is another's extremism. People don't go around calling themselves a fanatic, any more than they go around calling themselves Pimply. Would one also seek to reconcile slaves and slave masters, or persuade native peoples to complain only moderately about those who are plotting their extermination? What is the middle ground between racism and antiracism?

TERRY EAGLETON

If Marx had no time for the state, it was partly because he viewed it as a kind of alienated power. It was as though this august entity had confiscated the abilities of men and women to determine their own existence, and was now doing so on their behalf. It also had the impudence to call this process "democracy." Marx himself began his career as a radical democrat and ended up as a revolutionary one, as he came to realize just how much transformation genuine democracy would entail; and it is as a democrat that he challenges the state's sublime authority. He is too wholehearted a believer in popular sovereignty to rest content with the pale shadow of it known as parliamentary democracy. He is not in principle opposed to parliaments, any more than was Lenin. But he saw democracy as too precious to be entrusted to parliaments alone. It had to be local, popular and spread across all the institutions of civil society. It had to extend to economic as well as political life. It had to mean actual self-government, not government entrusted to a political elite. The state Marx approved of was the rule of citizens over themselves, not of a minority over a majority.

The state, Marx considered, had come adrift from civil society. There was a blatant contradiction between the two. We were, for example, abstractly equal as citizens within the state, but dramatically unequal in everyday social existence. That social existence was riven with conflicts, but the state projected an image of it as seamlessly whole. The state saw itself as shaping society from above, but was in fact a product of it. Society did not stem from the state; instead, the state was a parasite on society. The whole setup was topsy-turvy. As one commentator puts it, "Democracy and capitalism have been turned upside down"—meaning that instead of political institutions regulating capitalism, capitalism regulated them. The speaker is Robert Reich, a former U.S. labour secretary, who is not generally suspected of being a Marxist. Marx's aim was to close this gap between state and society, politics and everyday life, by dissolving the former into the latter. And this is what he called democracy. Men and women had to reclaim in their daily lives the powers that the state had appropriated from them. Socialism is the completion of democracy, not the negation of it. It is hard to see why so many defenders of democracy should find this vision objectionable.

It is a commonplace among Marxists that real power today lies with the banks, corporations and financial institutions, whose directors had never been elected by anyone, and whose decisions can affect the lives of millions. By and large, political power is the obedient servant of the Masters of the Universe. Governments might chide them from time to time, or even slap an Anti-Social Behavior Order on them; but if they sought to put them out of business they would be in dire danger of being clapped in prison themselves by their own security forces. At most, the state can hope to mop up some of the human damage the present system wreaks. It does so partly on humanitarian grounds, and partly to restore the system's tarnished credibility. This is what we know as social democracy. The fact that, generally speaking, politics is in hock to economics is the reason why the state as we know it cannot simply be hijacked for socialist ends. Marx writes in *The Civil War in France* that the working class cannot simply lay hands on the ready-made machinery of the state and wield it for its own purposes. This is because that machinery already has a built-in bias to the status quo. Its anaemic, woefully impoverished version of democracy suits the anti-democratic interests that currently hold sway.

Marx's main model for popular self-government was the Paris Commune of 1871, when for a few tumultuous months the working people of the French capital took command of their own destiny. The Commune, as Marx describes it in *The Civil War in France,* was made up of local councillors, mostly working men, who were elected by popular vote and could be recalled by their constituents. Public service had to be performed at workmen's wages, the standing army was abolished, and the police were made responsible to the Commune. The powers previously exercised by the French state were assumed instead by the Communards. Priests were banished from public life, while educational institutions were thrown open to the common people and freed of interference by both church and state. Magistrates, judges and public servants were to be elective, responsible to the people and recallable by them.

The Commune also intended to abolish private property in the name of cooperative production.

"Instead of deciding once in three or six years which member of the ruling class was to misrepresent the people in Parliament," Marx writes, "universal suffrage was to serve the people, constituted in Communes." The Commune, he goes on, "was essentially a working-class government ... the political form at last discovered under which to work out the economic emancipation of labour."[2] Though he was by no means uncritical of this ill-fated enterprise (he pointed out, for example, that most of the Communards were not socialists), he found in it many of the elements of a socialist politics. And it was from working-class practice, not from some theoretical drawing board, that this scenario had sprung. For a brief, enthralling moment, the state had ceased to be an alienated power and had taken instead the form of popular self-government.

What took place in those few months in Paris was what Marx describes as the "dictatorship of the proletariat." Few of his well-known phrases have sent more of a chill through the veins of his critics. Yet what he means by this sinister-sounding term was nothing more than popular democracy. The dictatorship of the proletariat meant simply rule by the majority. In any case, the word "dictatorship" in Marx's time did not necessarily suggest what it does today. It meant an extralegal breach of a political constitution. Marx's political sparring partner Auguste Blanqui, a man who had the distinction of being gaoled by every French government from 1815 to 1880, coined the phrase "dictatorship of the proletariat" to mean rule on behalf of the common people; Marx himself used it to mean government by them. Blanqui was elected president of the Paris Commune, but had to settle for the role of figurehead. As usual, he was in prison at the time.

There are times when Marx writes as though the state is simply a direct instrument of the ruling class. In his historical writings, however, he is usually a good deal more nuanced. The task of the political state is not just to serve the immediate interests of the governing class. It must also act to preserve social cohesion; and though these two goals are ultimately at one, there can be acute conflict between them in the short or middle term. Besides, the state under capitalism has more independence of class relations than it does under, say, feudalism. The feudal lord is both a political and an economic figure, whereas in capitalism these functions are usually distinguished. Your Member of Parliament is not generally your employer. This means that the capitalist state's appearance of being set above class relations is not *just* an appearance. How independent of material interests the state is depends on changing historical conditions. Marx seems to argue that in the so-called Asiatic mode of production, involving as it does vast irrigation works that only the state can establish, the state really is the dominant social force. So-called vulgar Marxists tend to assume a one-to-one relation between the state and the economically sovereign class, and there are occasions when this is actually the case. There are times when the possessing class directly runs the state. George Bush and his fellow oilmen were a case in point. One of Bush's most remarkable achievements, in other words, was to prove vulgar Marxism right. He also seems to have worked hard to make the capitalist system appear in the worst possible light, another fact which makes one wonder whether he was secretly working for the North Koreans.

The relations in question, however, are usually more complex than the Bush administration might suggest. (In fact, almost everything in human existence is more complex than it tended to suggest.) There are periods, for example, when one class rules on behalf of another. In nineteenth-century England, as Marx himself pointed out, the Whig aristocracy was still the governing political class, while the industrial middle class was increasingly the dominant economic one; and the former, generally speaking, represented the interests of the latter. Marx also argued that Louis Bonaparte ruled France in the interests of finance capitalism while presenting himself as a representative of the smallholding peasantry. Rather similarly, the Nazis ruled in the interests of high capitalism, but did so through an ideology which was distinctively lower-middle class in outlook. They could thus fulminate against upper-class parasites and the idle rich in ways which could be mistaken by the politically unwary as genuinely radical. Nor were the politically unwary wholly mistaken in this view. Fascism is indeed a form of radicalism. It has no time for liberal middle-class civilisation. It is just that it is a radicalism of the right rather than the left.

Unlike a great many liberals, Marx was not allergic to power as such. It is scarcely in the interests of the powerless to be told that all power is distasteful, not least by those who already have enough of the stuff to spare. Those to whom the word "power" always has a derogatory ring are fortunate indeed. Power in the cause of human emancipation is not to be confused with tyranny. The slogan "Black Power!" is a lot less feeble than the cry "Down with Power!" We would only know that such power was truly emancipatory, however, if it managed to transform not only the present political setup, but the very meaning of power itself. Socialism does not involve replacing one set of rulers with another. Speaking of the Paris Commune, Marx observes that "it was not a revolution to transfer [the state] from one fraction of the ruling class to another but a Revolution to break down this horrid machinery of Classdomination [*sic*] itself."[3]

Socialism involves a change in the very notion of sovereignty. There is only a dim resemblance between what the word "power" means in London today and what it meant in Paris in 1871. The most fruitful form of power is power over oneself, and democracy means the collective exercise of this capacity. It was the Enlightenment that insisted that the only form of sovereignty worth submitting to is one we have fashioned ourselves. Such self-determination is the most precious meaning of freedom. And though human beings may abuse their freedom, they are not fully human without it. They are bound to make rash or brainless decisions from time to time —decisions that a shrewd autocrat might well not have taken. But unless these decisions are *their* decisions, there is likely to be something hollow and inauthentic about them, however sagacious they may be.

So power survives from the capitalist present to the socialist future—but not in the same form. The idea of power itself undergoes a revolution. The same is true of the state. In one sense of the word "state," "state socialism" is as much a contradiction in terms as "the epistemological theories of Tiger Woods." In another sense, however, the term has some force. For Marx, there is still a state under socialism; only beyond socialism, under communism, will the coercive state give way to an administrative body. But it is not a state we ourselves would easily recognize as such. It is as though someone were to point to a decentralised network of self-governing communities, flexibly regulated by a democratically elected central administration, and announce "*There* is the state!," when we were expecting something altogether more imposing and monumental—something, for example, along the lines of Westminster, Whitehall and the mysteriously enigmatic Prince Andrew.

Part of Marx's quarrel with the anarchists was over the question of how fundamental power is in any case. Is it what ultimately matters? Not in Marx's opinion. For him, political power had to be set in a broader historical context. One had to ask what material interests it served, and it was these that in his view lay at the root of it. If he was critical of conservatives who idealized the state, he was also impatient with anarchists who overrated its importance. Marx refuses to "reify" power, severing it from its social surroundings and treating it as a thing in itself. And this is undoubtedly one of the strengths of his work. Yet it is accompanied, as strengths often are, by a certain blind spot. What Marx overlooks about power is what his compatriots Nietzsche and Freud both recognized in strikingly different ways. Power may not be a thing in itself; but there is an element within it which luxuriates in dominion simply for its own sake—which delights in flexing its muscles with no particular end in view, and which is always in excess of the practical goals to which it is harnessed. Shakespeare acknowledged this when he wrote of the relationship between Prospero and Ariel in *The Tempest*. Ariel is the obedient agent of Prospero's power, but he is restless to escape this sovereignty and simply do his own thing. In puckish, sportive spirit, he wants simply to relish his magical powers as ends in themselves, not have them tied down to his master's strategic purposes. To see power simply as instrumental is to pass over this vital feature of it; and to do so may be to misunderstand why power should be as formidably coercive as it is.

TEN

All the most interesting radical movements of the past four decades have sprung up from outside Marxism. Feminism, environmentalism, gay and ethnic politics, animal rights, antiglobalisation, the peace movement: these have now taken over from an antiquated commitment to class struggle, and represent new forms of political activism which have left Marxism well behind. Its contributions to them have been marginal and uninspiring. There is indeed still a political left, but it is one appropriate to a postclass, postindustrial world.

One of the most flourishing of the new political currents is known as the anticapitalist movement, so it is hard to see how there has been a decisive break with Marxism. However critical of Marxist ideas this movement might be, the shift from Marxism to anticapitalism is hardly a huge one. In fact, Marxism's dealings with other radical trends have been largely to its credit. Take, for example, its relations with the women's movement. These, to be sure, have proved fraught enough from time to time. Some male Marxists have contemptuously brushed aside the whole question of sexuality, or

211

sought to appropriate feminist politics for their own ends. There is plenty in the Marxist tradition that is at best complacently gender-blind and at worst odiously patriarchal. Yet this is far from being the whole story, as some separatist feminists in the 1970s and '80s liked self-servingly to suppose. Many male Marxists have learned enduringly from feminism, both personally and politically. And Marxism in turn has made a major contribution to feminist thought and practice.

Some decades ago, when the Marxist-feminist dialogue was at its most energetic, a whole set of vital questions were raised.[1] What was the Marxist view of domestic labour, which Marx himself had largely ignored? Did women form a social class in the Marxist sense? How was a theory largely concerned with industrial production to make sense of child care, consumption, sexuality, the family? Was the family central to capitalist society, or would capitalism herd people into communal barracks if it found it more profitable and could get away with it? (There is an assault on the middle-class family in the *Communist Manifesto,* a case which the philandering Friedrich Engels, eager to achieve a dialectical unity of theory and practice, zealously adopted in his private life.) Could there be freedom for women without the overthrow of class-society? What were the relations between capitalism and patriarchy, given that the latter is a great deal more ancient than the former? Some Marxist-feminists held that women's oppression could end only with the fall of capitalism. Others, perhaps more plausibly, claimed that capitalism could dispense with this mode of oppression and still survive. On this view, there is nothing in the nature of capitalism which requires the subjection of women. But the two histories, that of patriarchy and class-society, are so tightly interwoven in practice that it would be hard to imagine the overthrow of the one without great shock waves rolling through the other.

Much of Marx's own work is gender-blind—though this can sometimes be explained by the fact that capitalism is too, at least in certain respects. We have already noted the system's relative indifference to gender, ethnicity, social pedigree and so on when it comes to who it can exploit or to whom it can peddle its wares. If Marx's worker is eternally male, however, it is because Marx himself was an old-fashioned Victorian patriarch, not just because of the nature of capitalism. Even so, he sees sexually reproductive relations as of the first importance, and in *The German Ideology* even claims that to begin with the family is the only social relation. When it comes to the production of life itself—"both of one's own in labour and of fresh life in procreation"—the two grand historical narratives of sexual and material production, without either of which human history would grind rapidly to a halt, are seen by Marx as closely interwoven. What men and women create most notably are other men and women. In doing so, they generate the labour power that any social system needs to sustain itself. Both sexual and material reproduction have their own distinct histories, which are not to be merged into one; but both are sites of age-old strife and injustice, and their respective victims thus have a joint interest in political emancipation.

Engels, who practiced sexual as well as political solidarity with the proletariat by taking a working-class lover, thought the emancipation of women inseparable from the ending of class-society. (Since his lover was also Irish, he considerately added an anticolonial dimension to their relationship.) His work *The Origin of the Family, Private Property and the State* is an impressive piece of social anthropology, full of flaws but rife with good intentions, which while never challenging the conventional division of sexual labour, regards the oppression of women by men as "the first class subjection." The Bolsheviks took the so-called woman question equally seriously: the uprising that was to topple the Tsar was launched with mass demonstrations on International Women's Day in 1917. Once in power, the party gave equality for women a high political priority and set up an International Women's Secretariat. That Secretariat in turn summoned the First International Working Women's Congress, attended by delegates from twenty countries, whose appeal "To the Working Women of the World" viewed the goals of communism and the liberation of women as closely allied.

"Up until the resurgence of the women's movements in the 1960s," writes Robert J. C. Young, "it is striking how it was only men from the socialist or communist camps who regarded the issue of women's equality as intrinsic to other forms of political liberation."[2] In the early twentieth century, the communist movement was the only place where the issue of gender, along with questions of nationalism and colonialism, was systematically raised and debated. "Communism," Young continues, "was the first, and only, political programme to recognize the interrelation of these different forms of domination and exploitation [class, gender and colonialism] and the necessity of abolishing all of them as the fundamental basis for the successful realization of the liberation of each."[3] Most so-called socialist societies have pressed for substantial progress in women's rights, and many of them took the "woman question" with commendable seriousness long before the West got round to addressing it with any ardour. When it comes to issues of gender and sexuality, the actual record of communism has been seriously flawed; but it remains the case, as Michèle Barrett has argued, that "outside feminist thought there is no tradition of critical analysis of women's oppression that could match the incisive attention given to the question by one Marxist thinker after another."[4]

If Marxism has been a steadfast champion of women's rights, it has also been the most zealous advocate of the world's anticolonialist movements. It fact, throughout the first half of the twentieth century, it was the primary inspiration behind them. Marxists were thus in the van of the three greatest political struggles of the modern age: resistance to colonialism, the emancipation of women and the fight against fascism. For most of the great first-generation theorists of the anticolonial wars, Marxism provided the indispensable starting point. In the 1920s and '30s, practically the only men and women to be found preaching racial equality were communists. Most African nationalism after the Second World War, from Nkrumah and Fanon onwards, relied on some version of Marxism or socialism. Most communist parties in Asia incorporated nationalism into their agendas. As Jules Townshend writes:

> While the working classes, with the notable exceptions of the French and Italian, seemed to be relatively dormant in the advanced capitalist countries [in the 1960s], the peasantry, along with the intelligentsias, of Asia, Africa and Latin America were making revolutions, or creating societies, in the name of socialism. From Asia came the inspiration of Mao's Cultural Revolution in 1966 in China and Ho Chi Minh's Vietcong resistance to the Americans in Vietnam; from Africa the socialist and emancipatory visions of Nyerere of Tanzania, Nkrumah of Ghana, Cabral of Guinea-Bissau and Franz Fanon of Algeria; and from Latin America the Cuban Revolution of Fidel Castro and Che Guevara.[5]

TERRY EAGLETON

216

From Malaysia to the Caribbean, Ireland to Algeria, revolutionary nationalism forced Marxism to rethink itself. At the same time, Marxism sought to offer Third World liberation movements something rather more constructive than replacing rule by a foreign-based capitalist class with rule by a native one. It also looked beyond the fetish of the nation to a more internationalist vision. If Marxism lent its support to national liberation movements in the so-called Third World, it did so while insisting that their perspectives should be international-socialist rather than bourgeois-nationalist. For the most part, this insistence fell on deaf ears.

On coming to power, the Bolsheviks proclaimed the right of self-determination for colonial peoples. The world communist movement was to do an immense amount to translate this sentiment into practice. Lenin, despite his critical attitude to nationalism, had been the first major political theorist to grasp the significance of national liberation movements. He also insisted in the teeth of Romantic nationalism that national liberation was a question of radical democracy, not chauvinist sentiment. In a uniquely powerful combination, Marxism thus became both an advocate of anticolonialism and a critique of nationalist ideology. As Kevin Anderson comments, "Over three decades before India won its independence and more than four decades before the African liberation movements came to the fore in the early 1960s, [Lenin] was already theorizing anti-imperialist national movements as a major factor in global politics."[6] "All Communist Parties," Lenin wrote in 1920, "should render direct aid to the revolutionary movements among the dependent and under-privileged nations (for example Ireland, the American Negroes, etc.) and in the colonies."[7] He attacked what he called "Great Russian chauvinism" within the Soviet Communist Party, a stance that did not prevent him from effectively endorsing the annexation of the Ukraine and later the forcible absorption of Georgia. Some other Bolsheviks, including Trotsky and Rosa Luxemburg, displayed a strong hostility to nationalism.

Marx himself was somewhat more ambiguous about anticolonialist politics. In his early career, he tended to support the struggle against colonial power only if it seemed likely to promote the goal of socialist revolution. Certain nationalities, he scandalously declared, were "non-historic" and doomed to extinction. In a single Eurocentric gesture, Czechs, Slovenes, Dalmatians, Romanians, Croats, Serbs, Moravians, Ukrainians and others were cavalierly consigned to the ash can of history. At one point, Engels zealously supported the colonization of Algeria and the U.S. conquest of Mexico, while Marx himself had scant respect for the great Latin American liberator, Simon Bolivar. India, he remarks, could boast no history of its own, and its subjugation by the

British had unwittingly laid down the conditions for socialist revolution in the subcontinent. It is not the kind of talk that would land you an A in postcolonialism courses from Canterbury to California.

If Marx can speak positively about colonialism, it is not because he relishes the prospect of one nation trampling upon another. It is because he sees such oppression, vile and degrading as he judged it, as bound up with the arrival of capitalist modernity in the "undeveloped" world. This in turn he saw not only as bestowing certain benefits on that world, but also as preparing the way for socialism. We have already discussed the pros and cons of such "teleological" thought.

The suggestion that colonialism can have its progressive aspects tends to stick in the craw of most Western postcolonial writers, fearful as they are that to confess anything so politically incorrect might be to sell the pass to racism and ethnocentrism. It is, however, something of a commonplace among, say, Indian and Irish historians.[8] How could such a formidably complex phenomenon as colonialism, stretching as it does over a range of regions and centuries, have produced not a single positive effect? In nineteenth-century Ireland, British rule brought famine, violence, destitution, racial supremacy and religious oppression. It also brought in its wake much of the literacy, language, education, limited democracy, technology, communications and civic institutions which allowed the nationalist movement to organise and eventually seize power. These were valuable goods in themselves, as well as promoting a worthy political cause.

While a good many of the Irish were keen to enter upon the modern age by learning English, some upper-class Irish Romantics were patronizingly eager for them to speak nothing but their native tongue. We find a similar prejudice in some postcolonial writers today, for whom capitalist modernity would appear an unqualified disaster. It is not an opinion shared by many of the postcolonial peoples whose cause they champion. Of course it would have been preferable for the Irish to have entered upon democracy (and eventually prosperity) in some less traumatic way. The Irish should never have been reduced to the indignity of colonial subjects in the first place. Given that they were, however, it proved possible to pluck something of value from this condition.

Marx, then, may have detected some "progressive" trends in colonialism. But this did not stop him from denouncing the "barbarity" of colonial rule in India and elsewhere, or of cheering on the great Indian Rebellion of 1857. The alleged atrocities of the 1857 insurgents, he commented, were merely a reflex of Britain's own predatory conduct in the country. British imperialism in India, far from constituting a benignly civilising process, was "a bleeding process with a vengeance."[9] India laid bare the "profound hypocrisy and inherent barbarism of bourgeois civilisation," which assumed respectable guise at home but went naked abroad.[10] Indeed, Aijaz Ahmad claims that no influential nineteenth-century Indian reformer took as clear-cut a position as Marx did on the question of Indian national independence.[11]

Marx also recanted his earlier view of the conquest of Mexico, as Engels did of the French expropriation of Algeria. It had, the latter reflected bitterly, unleashed nothing but bloodshed, rapine, violence and the "barefaced arrogance" of the settlers on the "lesser breed" of natives. Only a revolutionary movement, Engels urged, would retrieve the situation. Marx championed the Chinese national liberation movement of his day against what he contemptuously called the colonialist "civilisation-mongers." He was, in other words, to make amends for his earlier chauvinism, rallying behind the liberation struggles of colonized nations whether they were "non-historic" or not. Assured that any nation that oppresses another forges its own chains, he viewed Irish independence as a precondition for socialist revolution in England. The conflict of the working class with their masters, he writes in the *Communist Manifesto,* at first takes the form of a national struggle.

For the tradition I have just traced, issues of culture, gender, language, otherness, difference, identity and ethnicity were inseparable from questions of state power, material inequality, the exploitation of labour, imperial plunder, mass political resistance and revolutionary transformation. If you were to subtract the latter from the former, however, you would have something like much of today's postcolonial theory. There is a simpleminded notion abroad that somewhere around 1980, a discredited Marxism gave way to a more politically relevant postcolonialism. This, in fact, involves what the philosophers call a category mistake, rather like trying to compare a dormouse with the concept of matrimony. Marxism is a mass political movement stretching across continents and centuries, a creed for which countless men and women have fought and sometimes died. Postcolonialism is an academic language largely unspoken outside a few hundred universities, and one sometimes as unintelligible to the average Westerner as Swahili.

As a theory, postcolonialism sprang into existence in the late twentieth century, around the time when the struggles for national liberation had more or less run their course. The founding work of the current, Edward Said's *Orientalism,* appeared in the mid-1970s, just as a severe crisis of capitalism was rolling back the revolutionary spirit in the West. It is perhaps significant in this respect that Said's book is quite strongly anti-Marxist. Postcolonialism, while preserving that revolutionary legacy in one sense, represents a displacement of it in another. It is a postrevolutionary discourse suitable to a postrevolutionary world. At its finest, it has produced work of rare insight and originality. At its least creditable, it represents little more than the foreign affairs department of postmodernism.

So it is not as though class must now give way to gender, identity and ethnicity. The conflict between the transnational corporations and the poorly paid, ethnic, often female labourers of the south of the globe *is* a question of class, in the precise Marxist sense of the term. It is not that a "Eurocentric" focus on, say, Western coal miners or mill workers has been now superseded by less provincial perspectives. Class was always an international phenomenon. Marx liked to think that it was the working class that acknowledged no homeland, but in reality it is capitalism. In one sense of the term, globalisation is stale news, as a glance at the *Communist Manifesto* would suggest. Women have always formed a large part of the labour force, and racial oppression was always hard to disentangle from economic exploitation. The so-called new social movements are for the most part not new at all. And the notion that they have "taken over" from a class-obsessed, antipluralist Marxism overlooks the fact that they and Marxism have worked in fruitful alliance for some considerable time.

Postmodernists have sometimes accused Marxism of being Eurocentric, seeking to impose its own white, rationalist Western values on very different sectors of the planet. Marx was certainly a European, as we can tell from his burning interest in political emancipation. Emancipatory traditions of thought mark the history of Europe, just as the practice of slavery does. Europe is the home of both democracy and the death camps. If it includes genocide in the Congo, it also encompasses the Paris Communards and the Suffragettes. It signifies both socialism and fascism, Sophocles and Arnold Schwarzenegger, civil rights and Cruise missiles, a legacy of feminism and a heritage of famine. Other parts of the globe are equally marked by a mixture of enlightened and oppressive practices. Only those who in their simpleminded way see Europe as wholly negative and the postcolonial "margins" as purely positive could overlook this fact. Some of them even call themselves pluralists. Most of these people are guilt-stricken Europeans rather than postcolonials with an animus against Europe. Their guilt rarely extends to the racism implicit in their contempt for Europe as such.

There is no doubt that Marx's work is limited by his social conditions. Indeed, if his own thought is valid, it could scarcely be otherwise. He was a middle-class European intellectual. But not many middle-class European intellectuals called for the overthrow of empire or the emancipation of factory workers. Indeed, a great many colonial intellectuals did not. Besides, it seems a touch patronizing to suggest that the whole brave band of anticolonial leaders who took up Marx's ideas, from James Connolly to C. L. R. James, were simply the deluded victims of Western Enlightenment. That mighty campaign for freedom, reason and progress, which sprang from the heart of middle-class eighteenth-century Europe, was both an enthralling liberation from tyranny and a subtle form of despotism in itself; and it was Marx above all who made us aware of this contradiction. He defended the great bourgeois ideals of freedom, reason and progress, but wanted to know why they tended to betray themselves whenever they were put into practice. He was thus a critic of Enlightenment—but like all the most effective forms of critique, his was from the inside. He was both its firm apologist and ferocious antagonist.

Those who are in search of political emancipation cannot afford to be too choosy about the pedigree of those who extend a hand to them. Fidel Castro did not turn his back on socialist revolution because Marx was a German bourgeois. Asian and African radicals have been stubbornly indifferent to the fact that Trotsky was a Russian Jew. It is usually middle-class liberals who fret about "patronising" working people by, say, lecturing to them about multiculturalism or William Morris. Working people themselves are generally free of such privileged neuroses, and are glad to receive whatever political support might seem useful. So it proved with those in the colonial world who first learnt about political freedom from Marx. Marx was indeed a European; but it was in Asia that his ideas first took root, and in the so-called Third World that they flourished most vigorously. Most so-called Marxist societies have been non-European. In any case, theories are never simply taken over and acted out by great masses of people; they are actively remade in the process. This, overwhelmingly, has been the story of Marxist anticolonialism.

Critics of Marx have sometimes noted a so-called Promethean strain in his work—a belief in Man's sovereignty over Nature, along with a faith in limitless human progress. There is indeed such a current in his writings, as one might expect from a nineteenth-century European intellectual. There was little concern with plastic bags and carbon emissions around 1860. Besides, Nature sometimes needs to be subjugated. Unless we build a lot of seawalls pretty quickly, we are in danger of losing Bangladesh. Typhoid jabs are an exercise of human sovereignty over Nature. So are bridges and brain surgery. Milking cows and building cities mean harnessing Nature to our own ends. The idea that we should never seek to get the better of Nature is sentimental nonsense. Yet even if we do need to get the better of it from time to time, we can do so only by that sensitive attunement to its inner workings known as science.

Marx himself sees this sentimentalism ("a childish attitude to nature," as he calls it) as reflecting a superstitious stance to the natural world, in which we bow down before it as a superior power; and this mystified relation to our surroundings reappears in modern times as what he calls the fetishism of commodities. Once again, our lives are determined by alien powers, dead bits of matter which have been imbued with a tyrannical form of life. It is just that these natural powers are no longer wood sprites and water nymphs but the movement of commodities on the market, over which we have as little control as Odysseus did over the god of the sea. In this sense as in others, Marx's critique of capitalist economics is closely bound up with his concern for Nature.

As early as *The German Ideology,* Marx is to be found including geographical and climatic factors in social analysis. All historical analysis, he declares, "must set out from these natural bases and their modification in the course of history through the action of men."[12] He writes in *Capital* of "socialised man, the associated producers, rationally regulating their material interchange with nature and bringing it under common control, instead of allowing it to rule them as a blind force."[13] "Interchange" rather than lordship, rational control rather than bullying dominion, is what is at stake. In any case, Marx's Prometheus (he was his favourite classical character) is less a bullish champion of technology than a political rebel. For Marx, as for Dante, Milton, Goethe, Blake, Beethoven and Byron, Prometheus represents revolution, creative energy and a revolt against the gods.[14]

The charge that Marx is just another Enlightenment rationalist out to plunder Nature in the name of Man is quite false. Few Victorian thinkers have so strikingly prefigured modern environmentalism. One modern-day commentator argues that Marx's work represents "the most profound insight into the complex issues surrounding the mastery over nature to be found anywhere in 19th century social thought or a fortiori in the contributions of earlier periods."[15] Even Marx's most loyal fans might find this claim a trifle overweening, though it contains a hefty kernel of truth. The young Engels was close to Marx's own ecological opinions when he wrote that "to make the earth an object of huckstering—the earth which is our one and all, the first condition of our existence—was the last step towards making oneself an object of huckstering."[16]

That the earth is the first condition of our existence—that if you want a foundation to human affairs, you might do worse than look for it there—is Marx's own claim in his *Critique of the Gotha Programme,* where he insists that it is Nature, not labour or production taken in isolation, which lies at the root of human existence. The older Engels writes in his *Dialectics of Nature* that "we by no means rule over nature like a conqueror over a foreign people, like someone standing outside nature—but we, with flesh, blood and brain, belong to nature, and exist in its midst, and all our mastery of it consists in the fact that we have the advantage over all other beings of being able to know and correctly apply its laws."[17] It is true that Engels also speaks in *Socialism: Utopian and Scientific* of humanity as the "real, conscious lord of nature." It is also true that he blotted his environmental copybook a little as a keen member of a Cheshire hunt, but it is a tenet of Marx's materialism that nothing and nobody is perfect.

"Even a whole society," Marx comments, "a nation, or even all simultaneously existing societies together, are not the owners of the globe. They are only its possessors, its usufructuaries, and like *boni patres familias* [good fathers of families] they must hand it down to succeeding generations in an improved condition."[18] He is well aware of the conflict between the short-term capitalist exploitation of natural resources and longer-term sustainable production. Economic advance, he insists again and again, must occur without jeopardizing the natural, global conditions on which the welfare of future generations depends. There is not the slightest doubt that he would have been in the forefront of the environmentalist movement were he alive today. As a protoecologist, he speaks of capitalism as "squandering the vitality of the soil" and working to undermine a "rational" agriculture.

"The rational cultivation of the soil as eternal communal property," Marx writes in *Capital,* is "an inalienable condition of the existence and reproduction of a chain of successive generations of the human race."[19] Capitalist agriculture, he considers, flourishes only by sapping the "original sources of all wealth . . . the soil and its labourers." As part of his critique of industrial capitalism, Marx discusses waste disposal, the destruction of forests, the pollution of rivers,

Why Marx Was Right

environmental toxins and the quality of the air. Ecological sustainability, he considered, would play a vital role in a socialist agriculture.[20]

Behind this concern for Nature lies a philosophical vision. Marx is a naturalist and materialist for whom men and women are part of Nature, and forget their creatureliness at their peril. He even writes in *Capital* of Nature as the "body" of humanity, "with which [it] must remain in constant interchange." The instruments of production, he comments, are "extended bodily organs." The whole of civilisation, from senates to submarines, is simply an extension of our bodily powers. Body and world, subject and object, should exist in delicate equipoise, so that our environment is as expressive of human meanings as a language. Marx calls the opposite of this "alienation," in which we can find no reflection of ourselves in a brute material world, and accordingly lose touch with our own most vital being.

When this reciprocity of self and Nature breaks down, we are left with the world of meaningless matter of capitalism, in which Nature is just pliable stuff to be cuffed into whatever shape we fancy. Civilisation becomes one vast cosmetic surgery. At the same time, the self is divorced from Nature, its own body and the bodies of others. Marx believes that even our physical senses have become "commodified" under capitalism, as the body, converted into a mere abstract instrument of production, is unable to savour its own sensuous life. Only through communism could we come to feel our own bodies again. Only then, he argues, can we move beyond a brutally instrumental reason and take delight in the spiritual and aesthetic dimensions of the world. Indeed, his work is "aesthetic" through and through. He complains in the *Grundrisse* that Nature under capitalism has become purely an object of utility, and has ceased to be recognized as a "power in itself."

Through material production, humanity in Marx's view mediates, regulates and controls the "metabolism" between itself and Nature, in a two-way traffic which is far from some arrogant supremacy. And all this—Nature, labour, the suffering, productive body and its needs—constitutes for Marx the abiding infrastructure of human history. It is the narrative that runs through and beneath human cultures, leaving its inescapable impress on them all. As a "metabolic" exchange between humanity and Nature, labour is in Marx's opinion an "eternal" condition which does not alter. What alters—what makes natural beings historical—are the various ways we humans go to work upon Nature. Humanity produces its means of subsistence in different ways. This is natural, in the sense that it is necessary for the reproduction of the species. But it is also cultural or historical, involving as it does specific kinds of sovereignty, conflict and exploitation. There is no reason to suppose that accepting the "eternal" nature of labour will deceive us into believing that these social forms are eternal as well.

This "everlasting nature-imposed condition of human existence," as Marx calls it, can be contrasted with the postmodern repression of the natural, material body, which it seeks to dissolve into culture. The very word "natural" provokes a politically correct shudder. All attention to our common biology becomes the thought crime of "biologism." Postmodernism is nervous of the unchanging, which it falsely imagines to be everywhere on the side of political reaction. So since the human body has altered little in the course of its evolution, postmodern thought can cope with it only as a "cultural construct." No thinker, as it happens, was more conscious than Marx of how Nature and the body are socially mediated. And that mediation is primarily known as labour, which works Nature up into human meaning. Labour is a signifying activity. We never bump into a brute piece of matter. Rather, the material world always comes to us shot through with human significance, and even blankness is one such signifier. The novels of Thomas Hardy illustrate this condition to superb effect.

The history of human society, Marx believes, is part of natural history. This means among other things that sociality is built into the kind of animals we are. Social cooperation is necessary for our material survival, but it is also part of our self-fulfillment as a species. So if Nature is in some sense a social category, society is also a natural one. Postmodernists are to be found insisting on the former but suppressing the latter. For Marx, the relation between Nature and humanity is not symmetrical. In the end, as he notes in *The German Ideology,* Nature has the upper hand. For the individual, this is known as death. The Faustian dream of progress without limits in a material world magically responsive to our touch overlooks "the priority of external nature." Today, this is known not as the Faustian dream but the American one. It is a vision which secretly detests the material because it blocks our path to the infinite. This is why the material world has either to be vanquished by force or dissolved into culture. Postmodernism and the pioneer spirit are sides of the same coin. Neither can accept that it is our limits that make us what we are, quite as much as that perpetual transgression of them we know as human history.

Human beings for Marx are part of Nature yet able to stand over against it; and this partial separation from Nature is itself part of their nature.[21] The very technology with which we set to work on Nature is fashioned from it. But though Marx sees Nature and culture as forming a complex unity, he refuses to dissolve the one into the other. In his alarmingly precocious early work, he dreams of an ultimate unity between Nature and humanity; in his more mature years, he recognizes that there will always be a tension or nonidentity between the two, and one name for this conflict is labour. No doubt with a certain regret, he rejects the beautiful fantasy, almost as old as humanity itself, in which an all-bountiful Nature is courteously deferential to our desires:

> What wondrous life is this I lead!
> Ripe apples drop about my head.
> The luscious clusters of the vine
> Upon my mouth do crush their wine.
> The nectarine and curious peach
> Into my hands themselves do reach;
> Stumbling on melons, as I pass,
> Insnared with flowers, I fall on grass.
>   (Andrew Marvell, "The Garden")

Marx believes in what he calls a "humanisation of nature"; but Nature in his view will always remain somewhat recalcitrant to humankind, even if its resistance to our needs can be diminished. And this has its positive aspect, since surmounting obstacles is part of our creativity. A magical world would also be a tedious one. One day in the magic garden would probably be enough for Marvell to wish he was back in London.

Did Marx believe in a boundless expansion of human powers, in a way offensive to our own ecological principles? It is true that he sometimes underplays the natural limits on human development, partly because opponents like Thomas Malthus overplayed them. He acknowledges the boundaries

Nature set on history, but thinks we could still push them a long way. There is certainly a marked strain of what we might call technological optimism—even, at times, triumphalism—in his work: a vision of the human race being borne on the back of unleashed forces of production into a brave new world. Some later Marxists (Trotsky was one of them) pushed this to a utopian extreme, foreseeing as they did a future stocked by heroes and geniuses.[22] But there is also another Marx, as we have seen already, who insists that such development should be compatible with human dignity and welfare. It is capitalism that sees production as potentially infinite, and socialism that sets it in the context of moral and aesthetic values. Or as Marx himself puts it in the first volume of *Capital,* "under a form appropriate to the full development of the human race."

Recognizing natural limits, as Ted Benton comments, is incompatible not with political emancipation but only with utopian versions of it.[23] The world has the resources not for us all to live better and better, but for us all to live well. "The promise of abundance," writes G. A. Cohen, "is not an endless flow of goods, but a sufficiency produced with a minimum of unpleasant exertion."[24] What prevents this from happening is not Nature but politics. For Marx, as we have seen, socialism requires an expansion of the productive forces; but the task of expanding them falls not to socialism itself but to capitalism. Socialism rides on the back of that material wealth, rather than building it up. It was Stalin, not Marx, who saw socialism as a matter of developing the productive forces. Capitalism is the sorcerer's apprentice: it has summoned up powers which have spun wildly out of control and now threaten to destroy us. The task of socialism is not to spur on those powers but to bring them under rational human control.

The two great threats to human survival that now confront us are military and environmental. They are likely to converge more and more in the future, as struggles over scarce resources escalate into armed conflict. Over the years, communists have been among the most ardent advocates of peace, and the reason for this is ably summarized by Ellen Meiksins Wood. "It seems to me axiomatic," she writes, "that the expansionary, competitive and exploitative logic of capitalist accumulation in the context of the nation-state system must, in the longer or shorter term, be destabilizing, and that capitalism . . . is and will for the foreseeable future remain the greatest threat to world peace."[25] If the peace movement is to grasp the root causes of global aggression, it cannot afford to ignore the nature of the beast that breeds it. And this means that it cannot afford to ignore the insights of Marxism.

The same goes for environmentalism. Wood argues that capitalism cannot avoid ecological devastation, given the anti-social nature of its drive to accumulate. The system may come to tolerate racial and gender equality, but it cannot by its nature achieve world peace or respect the material world. Capitalism, Wood comments, "may be able to accommodate some degree of ecological care, especially when the technology of environmental protection is itself profitably marketable. But the essential irrationality of the drive for capital accumulation, which subordinates everything to the requirements of the self-expansion of capital and so-called growth, is unavoidably hostile to ecological balance."[26] The old communist slogan "Socialism or barbarism" always seemed to some a touch too apocalyptic. As history lurches towards the prospect of nuclear warfare and environmental catastrophe, it is hard to see how it is less than the sober truth. If we do not act now, it seems that capitalism will be the death of us.

Conclusion

So there we have it. Marx had a passionate faith in the individual and a deep suspicion of abstract dogma. He had no time for the concept of a perfect society, was wary of the notion of equality, and did not dream of a future in which we would all wear boiler suits with our National Insurance numbers stamped on our backs. It was diversity, not uniformity, that he hoped to see. Nor did he teach that men and women were the helpless playthings of history. He was even more hostile to the state than right-wing conservatives are, and saw socialism as a deepening of democracy, not as the enemy of it. His model of the good life was based on the idea of artistic self-expression. He believed that some revolutions might be peacefully accomplished, and was in no sense opposed to social reform. He did not focus narrowly on the manual working class. Nor did he see society in terms of two starkly polarized classes.

He did not make a fetish of material production. On the contrary, he thought it should be done away with as far as possible. His ideal was leisure, not labour. If he paid such unflagging attention to the economic, it was in order to diminish its power over humanity. His materialism was fully compatible with deeply held moral and spiritual convictions. He lavished praise on the middle class, and saw socialism as the inheritor of its great legacies of liberty, civil rights and material prosperity. His views on Nature and the environment were for the most part startlingly in advance of his time. There has been no more staunch champion of women's emancipation, world peace, the fight against fascism or the struggle for colonial freedom than the political movement to which his work gave birth.

Was ever a thinker so travestied?

Notes

PREFACE

1. Peter Osborne, in Leo Panich and Colin Leys (eds.), *The Communist Manifesto Now: Socialist Register* (New York, 1998), p. 190.

2. Quoted by Robin Blackburn, "Fin de Siècle: Socialism after the Crash," *New Left Review,* no. 185 (January/February 1991), p. 7.

CHAPTER ONE

1. Though some Marxists doubt how vital they were. Alex Callinicos, for example, in *Against Postmodernism* (Cambridge, 1989), Ch. 5.

2. Fredric Jameson, *The Ideologies of Theory* (London, 2008), p. 514.

3. Tristram Hunt, "War of the Words," *Guardian,* 9 May 2009.

CHAPTER TWO

1. See Joseph Stiglitz, *Globalisation and Its Discontents* (London, 2002), p. 5.

2. Quoted in Slavoj Žižek, *First as Tragedy, Then as Farce* (London, 2009), p. 91.

3. Isaac Deutscher, *The Prophet Armed: Trotsky 1879–1921* (London, 2003), p. 373.

4. See, for example, Alec Nove, *The Economics of Feasible Socialism* (London, 1983), David Schweickart, *Against Capitalism* (Cambridge, 1993), and Bertell Ollman (ed.), *Market Socialism: The Debate Among Socialists* (New York and London, 1998). A more philosophical defence of market socialism is to be found in David Miller, *Market, State and Community: The Theoretical Foundations of Market Socialism* (Oxford, 1989).

5. Melvin Hill (ed.), *Hannah Arendt: The Recovery of the Public World* (New York, 1979), pp. 334–35.

6. Quoted by Robin Blackburn, "Fin de Siècle: Socialism after the Crash," *New Left Review,* no. 185 (January/February 1991), p. 29.

7. See, for example, *Pat Devine, Democracy and Economic Planning* (Cambridge, 1988), David McNally, *Against the Market* (London, 1993), and Michael Albert, *Parecon: Life After Capitalism* (London, 2003). A useful summary of this case is to be found in Alex Callinicos, *An Anti-Capitalist Manifesto* (Cambridge, 2003), Ch. 3.

8. See Ernest Mandel, "The Myth of Market Socialism," *New Left Review,* no. 169 (May/June 1988), p. 109 n.

9. Devine, *Democracy and Economic Planning,* pp. 253, 265–66.

10. Albert, *Parecon,* p. 59.

11. Raymond Williams, *Communications* (Harmondsworth, 1962).

CHAPTER THREE

1. Quoted in Alex Callinicos (ed.), *Marxist Theory* (Oxford, 1989), p. 143.

2. Marx, Preface to *A Contribution to the Critique of Political Economy,* in *Marx and Engels: Selected Works* (London, 1968), p. 182.

3. The most effective defence of the theory is to be found in G. A. Cohen, *Marx's Theory of History: A Defence* (Oxford, 1978). Rarely has a

wrongheaded idea been so magnificently championed. For an excellent account of Marx's theory of history, see S. H. Rigby, *Marxism and History* (Manchester and New York, 1987), a work I have drawn upon here.

4. Quoted in Alex Callinicos and Chris Harmon, *The Changing Working Class* (London, 1983), p. 13.

5. Marx, *The Holy Family* (New York, 1973), p. 101.

6. Marx & Engels, *Selected Correspondence* (Moscow, 1975), pp. 390–91.

7. Ibid., pp. 293–94.

8. A point made by John Maguire, *Marx's Theory of Politics* (Cambridge, 1978), p. 123.

9. Marx, *Capital,* vol. 1 (New York, 1967), p. 9.

10. Quoted in T. Bottomore (ed.), *A Dictionary of Marxist Thought* (Oxford, 1983), p. 140.

11. Quoted in Umberto Melotti, *Marxism and the Third World* (London, 1972), p. 6.

12. Marx, *Theories of Surplus Value* (London, 1972), p. 134.

13. Quoted in Alfred Schmidt, *The Concept of Nature in Marx* (London, 1971), p. 36.

14. Aijaz Ahmad, *In Theory: Classes, Nations, Literatures* (London, 1992), p. 228.

CHAPTER FOUR

1. For one of the finest studies of the more positive meanings of the idea, see Fredric Jameson, *Archaeologies of the Future* (London, 2005).

2. Marx and Engels, *The German Ideology* (London, 1974).

3. Marx, *The Civil War in France* (New York, 1972), p. 134.

4. Raymond Williams, *Culture and Society 1780–1950* (Harmondsworth, 1985), p. 320.

5. Norman Geras, *Marx and Human Nature: Refutation of a Legend* (London, 1983).

6. Terry Eagleton, *The Illusions of Postmodernism* (Oxford, 1996), p. 47.

7. See Len Doyal and Roger Harris, "The Practical Foundations of Human Understanding," *New Left Review,* no. 139 (May/June 1983).

8. For a counterargument, see Eagleton, *The Illusions of Postmodernism.*

9. Norman Geras, "The Controversy about Marx and Justice," *New Left Review,* no. 150 (March/April 1985), p. 82.

10. Quoted by Norman Geras, "The Controversy about Marx and Justice," *New Left Review,* no. 150 (March/April 1985), p. 52.

CHAPTER FIVE

1. John Gray, *False Dawn: The Delusions of Global Capitalism* (London, 2002), p. 12.

2. Marx and Engels, *Selected Correspondence* (Moscow, 1965), p. 417.

3. Theodor W. Adorno, *Negative Dialectics* (London, 1966), p. 320.

4. Jean-Jacques Rousseau, *A Discourse on Inequality* (London, 1984), p. 122.

5. John Elliot Cairnes, "Mr Comte and Political Economy," *Fortnightly Review* (May 1870).

6. W. E. H. Lecky, *Political and Historical Essays* (London, 1908), p. 11.

7. Arthur Friedman (ed.), *Collected Works of Oliver Goldsmith* (Oxford, 1966), vol. 2, p. 338.

8. For an excellent discussion of this point, see Peter Osborne, *Marx* (London, 2005), Ch. 3.

9. Marx, *Theories of Surplus Value* (London, 1972), p. 202.

10. Marx, *Economic and Philosophical Manuscripts of 1844,* in *Selected Works of Marx and Engels* (New York, 1972).

11. Marx, *Grundrisse* (Harmondsworth, 1973), pp. 110–11.

12. Marx, *Capital* (New York, 1967), vol. 1, p. 85.

CHAPTER SIX

1. Etienne Balibar, *The Philosophy of Marx* (London, 1995), p. 2.

2. Quoted in Alfred Schmidt, *The Concept of Nature in Marx* (London, 1971), p. 24.

3. Ibid., p. 26.

4. Ibid., p. 25.

5. Jürgen Habermas, *Knowledge and Human Interests* (Oxford, 1987), p. 35.

6. Marx and Engels, *The German Ideology* (London, 1974), p. 151.

7. See Alex Callinicos, *The Revolutionary Ideas of Karl Marx* (London and Sydney, 1983), p. 31.

8. Marx and Engels, *The German Ideology,* p. 51.

9. A phrase which does not of course mean "to raise too many questions." Readers who think it does are referred to the *Oxford English Dictionary*.

10. John Macmurray, *The Self as Agent* (London, 1957), p. 101.

11. Quoted by Jon Elster, *Making Sense of Marx* (Cambridge, 1985), p. 64.

12. For two interesting studies of the relations between the two thinkers, see David Rubinstein, *Marx and Wittgenstein: Knowledge, Morality and Politics* (London, 1981), and G. Kitching and Nigel Pleasants (eds.), *Marx and Wittgenstein* (London, 2006).

13. Marx and Engels, *The German Ideology,* p. 47.

14. In his *Notes on Wagner*, Marx speaks in strikingly Freudian terms of human beings first distinguishing objects in the world in terms of pain and pleasure, and then learning to distinguish which of them satisfy needs and which do not. Knowledge, as with Nietzsche, begins as a form of mastery over these objects. It is thus associated by both Marx and Nietzsche with power.

15. William Empson, *Some Versions of Pastoral* (London, 1966), p. 114.

16. Theodor Adorno, *Prisms* (London, 1967), p. 260.

17. Hannah Arendt (ed.), *Walter Benjamin: Illuminations* (London, 1973), pp. 256–57.

18. Marx, Preface to *A Contribution to the Critique of Political Economy,* in *Marx and Engels: Selected Works* (London, 1968), p. 182.

19. G. A. Cohen, *History, Labour and Freedom* (Oxford, 1988), p. 178.

20. See S. H. Rigby, *Engels and the Formation of Marxism* (Manchester, 1992), p. 233.

21. For an excellent biography of Marx, see Francis Wheen, *Karl Marx* (London, 1999).

22. See Max Beer, *Fifty Years of International Socialism* (London, 1935), p. 74. I am grateful to Marc Mulholland for this reference.

23. Quoted in Tom Bottomore (ed.), *Interpretations of Marx* (Oxford, 1988), p. 275.

CHAPTER SEVEN

1. Perry Anderson, *The Origins of Postmodernity* (London, 1998), p. 85.

2. See Mike Davis, *Planet of Slums* (London, 2006), p. 25.

3. Marx, *Contribution to the Critique of Hegel's Philosophy of Right,* in *Marx and Engels: Selected Works* (London, 1968), p. 219.

4. Quoted in Leo Panitch and Colin Leys (eds.), *The Socialist Register* (New York, 1998), p. 68.

5. I have drawn for the account which follows on (among other sources) Alex Callinicos and Chris Harman, *The Changing Working Class* (London and Melbourne, 1987); Lindsey German, *A Question of Class* (London, 1996); and Chris Harman, "The Workers of the World," *International Socialism,* no. 96 (autumn, 2002).

6. Jules Townshend, *The Politics of Marxism* (London and New York, 1996), p. 237.

7. Quoted by Tom Bottomore (ed.), *Interpretations of Marx* (Oxford, 1968), p. 19.

8. John Gray, *False Dawn: The Delusions of Global Capitalism* (London, 2002), p. 111.

9. Chris Harman, "The Workers of the World." For a contrary case about the working class, see G. A. Cohen, *If You're an Egalitarian, How Come You're So Rich?* (London, 2000).

10. See Perry Anderson, *New Left Review,* no. 48 (November/December 2007), p. 29.

11. For the enlightenment of readers unfamiliar with British upper-class crime, Lord Lucan is or was an English aristocrat who is alleged to have murdered his au pair and who disappeared without trace some decades ago.

12. A point made by Slavoj Žižek in *In Defense of Lost Causes* (London, 2008), p. 425. For a superb account of today's slums, see Mike Davis, *Planet of Slums* (London, 2006).

CHAPTER EIGHT

1. Isaac Deutscher, *Stalin* (Harmondsworth, 1968), p. 173.

2. G. K. Chesterton, *Orthodoxy* (New York, 1946), p. 83.

3. In the militant 1970s, the purity of a socialist's beliefs was sometimes assessed by his or her answer to such questions as "Would you use the bourgeois law courts if your partner was murdered?" or "'Would you write for the bourgeois press?" The true purists or ultraleftists, however, were those who were able to return an unequivocal No to the question "Would you call the bourgeois fire brigade?"

4. Quoted in Christopher Hill, *God's Englishman: Oliver Cromwell and the English Revolution* (London, 1990), p. 137.

CHAPTER NINE

1. Jacques Rancière, *Dis-agreement* (Minneapolis, 1999), p.113.

2. Marx, *The Civil War in France* (New York, 1972), p. 213.

3. Quoted in Tom Bottomore, *Interpretations of Marx* (Oxford, 1988), p. 286.

CHAPTER TEN

1. For a flavour of these debates, see Juliet Mitchell, *Women's Estate* (Harmondsworth, 1971); S. Rowbotham, L. Segal and H. Wainwright, *Beyond the Fragments* (Newcastle and London, 1979); L. Sargent (ed.), *Women and Revolution* (Montreal, 1981); and Michèle Barrett, *Women's Oppression Today* (revised edition, London, 1986).

2. Robert J. C. Young, *Postcolonialism: An Historical Introduction* (Oxford, 2001), pp. 372–73.

3. Ibid., p. 142.

4. Michèle Barrett, in T. Bottomore (ed.), *A Dictionary of Marxist Thought* (Oxford, 1983), p. 190.

5. Jules Townshend, *The Politics of Marxism* (London and New York, 1996), p. 142.

6. Kevin B. Anderson, "The Rediscovery and Persistence of the Dialectic in Philosophy and in World Politics," in *Lenin Reloaded: Towards a Politics of Truth,* ed. S. Budgeon, S. Kouvelakis and S. Žižek (London, 2007), p. 121.

7. Quoted in ibid., p. 133.

8. For Indian historiography, see Aijaz Ahmad, *In Theory: Classes, Nations, Literatures* (London, 1992), Ch. 6.

9. Quoted by Ahmad, *In Theory,* p. 228.

10. Quoted in ibid., p. 235.

11. Ibid., p. 236.

12. Marx and Engels, *German Ideology,* p. 33.

13. Marx, *Capital,* vol. 3 (New York, 1967), p. 102.

14. John Bellamy Foster, "Marx and the Environment," in *In Defense of History,* ed. E. M. Wood and J. B. Foster (New York, 1997), p. 150.

15. W. Leiss, *The Domination of Nature* (Boston, 1974), p. 198.

16. Quoted in ibid., p. 153.

17. Frederick Engels, *The Dialectics of Nature* (New York, 1940), pp. 291–92.

18. Marx, *Capital,* vol. 3, p. 218.

19. Ibid., p. 219.

20. See Ted Benton, "Marxism and Natural Limits," *New Left Review,* no. 178 (November/December 1989), p. 83.

21. For a classic account of Marx's ideas on this subject, see Alfred Schmidt, *The Concept of Nature in Marx* (London, 1971).

22. See, for example, the closing paragraphs of Trotsky's *Literature and Revolution.*

23. Benton, "Marxism and Natural Limits," p. 78.

24. G. A. Cohen, *Karl Marx's Theory of History: A Defence* (Oxford, 1978), p. 307.

25. Ellen Meiksins Wood, "Capitalism and Human Emancipation," *New Left Review,* no. 67 (January/February 1988), p. 5.

26. Ibid., p. 5.

Index

Why Marx Was Right

future: evolutionist view of, 72–73; as
failure of the present, 79; faith in,
98; foretelling, 65–67; inevitability
of, 65–67; starting with the present, 71–73, 79, 100, 102

Geras, Norman, 80, 101
Germany: Nazi Party in, 99, 206–7;
unification of, 58
Giddens, Anthony, 35
globalisation, 3, 4, 223
Goldsmith, Oliver, 118–19; "The
Deserted Village," 31–32
Gray, John, 108, 174
greed, 5, 16, 96
Greenspan, Alan, 97
Guevara, Che, 216

Habermas, Jürgen, 136
Hardy, Thomas, 154, 232
Harman, Chris, 175
harmony, 200
Harvey, David, 170
Hegel, Georg Wilhelm Friedrich, 31,
200
history: alternative, 63; break with,
73; class struggle in, 33, 34–36, 50,
92, 119–20; consistency in, 112;
discontinuities in, 51; economic
theory of, 110, 116, 119; Enlightenment view of, 56; evolution of, 54–
56, 60; goldfish theory of, 73;
grand narrative of, 112; hierarchies in, 109; human misery in,
61; and human nature, 70; Marx's
theory of, 30, 34, 35, 40, 41, 50, 56–
57, 59, 61, 115–16, 122–23, 243n3;
Marx's use of term, 35, 115; material pressures in, 98–99, 115; moral

progress in, 93; moving towards
perfection, 67; Nature in, 54; patterns of, 110–11; plurality of forces
in, 108–10; productive forces in,
44; random events in, 52, 55–56;
teleological theory of, 59–60
Hitler, Adolf, 99
Ho Chi Minh, 216
Homer, 150
Horkheimer, Max, 61
human nature, 79–86, 97, 99–100,
123, 124; and history, 70; and labour, 120–21; and materialism,
130, 132, 137–38
Hume, David, 137
Hunt, Tristram, 9

India: as British colony, 218–19, 220;
independence of, 217, 220–21
Indian Rebellion (1857), 220–21
individualism, 129
information society, 173
Ireland: as British colony, 219–20;
Dublin uprising (1916), 180; Great
Irish Famine, 185; independence
of, 221; and Northern Ireland, 93–
94, 182; Ulster Unionists in, 189–
90

James, C. L. R., 224
Jameson, Fredric, 8
Jefferson, Thomas, 22

knowledge, 143; tacit, 147

labour: anthropology of, 120–21; as
basis of culture, 107; as basis of
wealth, 126; in history, 111–12;
and praxis, 125

Why Marx Was Right

Why Marx Was Right